# AQA
## GERMANY 1919–1945
## FOR SHP GCSE

**Dale Banham**
**Christopher Culpin**

DYNAMIC
LEARNING

HODDER
EDUCATION
AN HACHETTE UK COMPANY

**Acknowledgements**

**Photo credits**

**Cover** © Bettmann/Corbis; **p.i** © Bettmann/Corbis; **p.2** © bpk/Bayerische Staatsbibliothek/Heinrich Hoffmann; **p.6** © bpk; **p.7** © akg-images; **p.10** *bl* © Süddeutsche Zeitung Photo/SZ Photo; **p.12** *t* © bpk, *b* © akg-images; **p.13** *t* © Ullsteinbild/TopFoto, *b* © bpk/Heinrich Hoffmann; **p.15** *t & b* © Bettman/Corbis; **p.18** © Süddeutsche Zeitung Photo/SZ Photo; **p.27** © akg-images; **p.29** *t* © Ullsteinbild/TopFoto, *b* © akg-images; **p.31** © Ullsteinbild/TopFoto; **p.39** © bpk/ Bayerische Staatsbibliothek/Heinrich Hoffmann; **p.50** *t* © ullstein bild–Frentz, *b* © akg-images; **p.51** *l* © 2008 IBL Collections/Mary Evans Picture Library, *r* © akg-images; **p.53** © Ullsteinbild/TopFoto; **p.54** *tr & bl* © akg-images; **p.55** © Ullsteinbild/TopFoto; **p.56** © Ullsteinbild/TopFoto; **p.57** © Sueddeutsche Zeitung Photo/Scherl; **p.60** © Bundesarchiv, Plak 003-002-046, Graphiker: René Ahrlé; **p.62** © akg-images; **p.63** © bpk; **p.64** *l* © Bundesarchiv, Plak 003-002-046, Graphiker: René Ahrlé, *r* © Bildarchiv Preussischer Kulturbesitz; **p.65** *t* © Bundesarchiv Koblenz, Bild 146-1969-062A-62, Fotograf: o. Ang., *b* © Hulton-Deutsch Collection/CORBIS; **p.66** © Institut fur Stadtgeschichte, Frankfurt am Main; **p.67** *l* © bpk/Germin, *r* © Süddeutsche Zeitung Photo/Scherl; **p.69** © Popperfoto/Getty Images; **p.71** *tl* © Süddeutsche Zeitung Photo/Scherl, *tc* © bpk/Arthur Grimm, *br* © Bundesarchiv, Bild 146-1973-060-19, Fotograf: o.Ang.; **p.76** *l* © akg-images, *r* © World History Archive/Alamy; **p.78** *t* © Image bank WW2 – Netherlands Institute for War Documentation, *b* © akg-images/Michael Teller; **p.79** © United States Holocaust Memorial Museum, courtesy of Samuel Gruber; **p.82** © INTERFOTO/Alamy; **p.83** *t* © akg-images, *b* © Süddeutsche Zeitung Photo/Scherl; **p.84** *tr* © Ullsteinbild/TopFoto, *bl* © Keystone/Getty Images; **p.85** *tr & bl* © akg-images; **p.86** © Bettmann/Corbis; **p.87** © ullsteinbild/ TopFoto.

**Text credits**

**p.15** K. Heiden, *Der Führer: Hitler's Rise to Power* (Pordes, 1967); **p.38** E. A Buller, *Darkness over Germany* (Longman, 1943); **p.78** Rudolph Höss, *Death Dealer: The Memoirs of the SS Kommandant at Auschwitz* (DaCapo Press, 1996).

**The Schools History Project**

Set up in 1972 to bring new life to history for students aged 13–16, the Schools History Project continues to play an innovatory role in secondary history education. From the start, SHP aimed to show how good history has an important contribution to make to the education of a young person. It does this by creating courses and materials which both respect the importance of up-to-date, well-researched history and provide enjoyable learning experiences for students.

Since 1978 the Project has been based at Trinity and All Saints University College Leeds. It continues to support, inspire and challenge teachers through the annual conference, regional courses and website: www.schoolshistoryproject.org.uk. The Project is also closely involved with government bodies and awarding bodies in the planning of courses for Key Stage 3, GCSE and A level.

Every effort has been made to trace all copyright holders, but if any have been inadvertently overlooked the Publishers will be pleased to make the necessary arrangements at the first opportunity.

Although every effort has been made to ensure that website addresses are correct at time of going to press, Hodder Education cannot be held responsible for the content of any website mentioned in this book. It is sometimes possible to find a relocated web page by typing in the address of the home page for a website in the URL window of your browser.

Hachette UK's policy is to use papers that are natural, renewable and recyclable products and made from wood grown in sustainable forests. The logging and manufacturing processes are expected to conform to the environmental regulations of the country of origin.

Orders: please contact Bookpoint Ltd, 130 Milton Park, Abingdon, Oxon OX14 4SB. Telephone: +44 (0)1235 827720. Fax: +44 (0)1235 400454. Lines are open 9.00a.m.–5.00p.m., Monday to Saturday, with a 24-hour message answering service. Visit our website at www.hoddereducation.co.uk.

Typeset in 11/13 pt Palatino Light
Layouts by Ian Foulis and DC Graphic Design Limited
Artwork by Art Construction, Richard Duszczak, Jon Davis/Linden Artists, Janek Matysiak, Tony Randell, Steve Smith
Printed and bound in Dubai

A catalogue record for this title is available from the British Library

ISBN 978 1 444 12312 8

# Contents

# Introduction: What is an Enquiry in Depth?

You probably recognise the man in the middle of this picture, the focus of everyone's attention: Adolf Hitler. He became ruler of Germany in 1933 and remained in power until 1945. The people in the picture seem to be very pleased with him. Yet Hitler eventually hurtled Germany into war and murdered millions of people. By 1945 his country was in ruins and his people were starving.

How could this happen? How could the intelligent, educated people of a modern, democratic country let Hitler take over? And what happened to them once he had? These are the **big questions** that you are going to answer in this book. To answer them you need to study the period in some depth. That is why this is called an Enquiry in Depth.

An Enquiry in Depth:

- concentrates on a short period of history – in this case 27 years, from 1919 to 1945
- looks at *one* particular place at that time – in this case Germany
- looks at the lives of ordinary people (children, women and men) – not just at famous or powerful people
- studies people's feelings and motives – what made them tick and why they did what they did.

As you can see from the diagram below, the Enquiry in Depth forms a very important part of your GCSE History course.

## How does your GCSE History course all fit together?

Your GCSE History course may look like a random set of topics, but it's not like that at all. The course was designed to let you investigate different types, topics and periods of history. This is much more varied and interesting than sticking to just one period throughout your course.

| HISTORY AROUND US (25%) | STUDY IN DEVELOPMENT (35%) | ENQUIRY IN DEPTH (40%) |
|---|---|---|
| This investigation of a historical site in your locality lets you use different kinds of sources and contrasts with the national and international history in the other units. | This unit shows the value of developing a long overview of a topic. | This investigation of a short period of time allows you to develop an in-depth understanding of a topic. It offers a contrast to the much longer Study in Development. |

# What are the best ways to prepare for your GCSE exams?

Good revision and planning will help you do well at GCSE. We will help you using the two important features below.

 **smarter revision**

## The Smarter Revision Toolkit

The toolkit helps you prepare your revision notes thoroughly and intelligently. Each tool helps you with an aspect of your revision.

**Acronyms** – help you remember key details. See page 20.

**Concept map** – helps you to link different events together and to improve your explanations. See page 17.

**Memory map** – helps you remember key features and events of a period. See pages 20–21.

**Living graph** – helps you see the patterns of change. See page 45.

**SMARTER REVISION TOOLKIT**

**Summary table** – helps you evaluate the extent of change across a period. See page 92.

**Flash cards** – help you organise your revision notes. See page 87.

**Annotated pictures** – help trigger your memory about key changes that take place. See page 92.

 **meet the examiner**

These pages will:

- advise you how to write good answers and how to avoid writing bad answers
- show you sample answers and ask you to evaluate and improve them
- set you sample questions to improve your skills at writing good answers.

They will also explain how to answer the main types of exam questions. For example:

- Using Sources questions – these ask you to:
  - develop inferences from a source (see pages 26–27)
  - cross-reference sources – looking for similarities and differences between them (see page 57)
  - explain why different sources provide different views (see page 57)
  - evaluate the usefulness of a source (see page 89).
- questions that require you to use your own knowledge to:
  - explain why an event, person or group was important (see page 73)
  - explain the causes of an event (see pages 18–19)
  - evaluate the importance of a range of factors (see pages 43, 80–81).

## 1.1 What problems did the Weimar Republic face?

Germany emerged from its defeat in the First World War with a new government, called the Weimar Republic. It faced a lot of serious problems. It only just survived. Your task will be to examine these problems and decide which was the most threatening.

### Why did Germany need a new government in 1918?

Since 1888 Germany had been ruled by Kaiser (Emperor) Wilhelm II. Although Germany had a parliament, called the Reichstag, it was the Kaiser, a **strong leader**, who had most of the power. He chose ministers to help him run the country. He made sure that they would do what he wanted. If they did not, he would sack them.

By the autumn of 1918 the Kaiser was in big trouble. For four years Germany had been fighting in the First World War. It now faced certain defeat. The German army was retreating and people in Germany faced starvation.

The Allies (Britain, France and the USA) would only make peace with Germany if it became more democratic. This meant getting rid of the Kaiser and setting up a new government. Throughout Germany there were violent uprisings against the Kaiser. Eventually, he was forced to flee to the Netherlands. Germany became a republic.

Friedrich Ebert became the new democratically elected leader of Germany. Ebert was leader of the Social Democrats, the largest party in the Reichstag.

# How was the Weimar Republic governed?

In 1919 there was a general election. Friedrich Ebert became the President. There was too much violence in Berlin, the capital, for the new government to meet there, so it met in the town of Weimar. The government was therefore called the Weimar Republic.

During 1919 a new constitution was drawn up. This was a set of rules for how Germany would be governed. As you can see from the diagram below, it was very different to the old system, under the Kaiser. In fact, the Weimar constitution was one of the most democratic systems of government in the world.

## THE WEIMAR CONSTITUTION

### THE PRESIDENT
- Elected every seven years
- Controlled the armed forces
- Stayed out of the day-to-day running of the country
- In an emergency he could make laws without going through the Reichstag (parliament)

**appointed** ⬇

### THE CHANCELLOR
- Responsible for the day-to-day running of the country
- Chosen from the Reichstag by the President
- Like a prime minister

**needed the support of more than half of** ⬇

### THE REICHSTAG (parliament)
- Voted on new laws
- Members elected every four years, through a system called PR (proportional representation). This system gave small parties a chance to have a say in parliament

**was elected by** ⬇

### THE GERMAN PEOPLE
- Elected the President and the members of the Reichstag
- All men and women over the age of 20 could vote
- All adults had equal rights and the right of free speech

**Discuss**

1 What do you like about the Weimar constitution?
2 What weaknesses can you see in it?
3 What differences can you spot between the way the Weimar Republic was governed and the way the country you live in is governed?

## Coming up …

This constitution looks promising, doesn't it? Unfortunately for the new Weimar Republic it was set up at a very difficult time. As you will see in the rest of this section, the new Republic faced serious problems.

# Problems, problems, problems!

You are now going to study, in detail, five problems that the Weimar Republic faced. Do not think that each problem went away as another appeared. In fact, new problems combined with old problems. More and more problems built up. Together these problems threatened to destroy the Weimar Republic.

It was the end of the First World War that set the ball rolling …

On the next ten pages you will analyse the problems which combined to weaken the Weimar Republic. On pages 16–17 you will assess the importance of each problem and show the links between them.

## PROBLEM 1: DEFEAT IN THE FIRST WORLD WAR – THE 'STAB IN THE BACK'

Within days of taking over, the new government had to sign an armistice that ended the fighting in the First World War. The leaders of the Republic had little choice but to sign this – the German army was retreating and people at home faced starvation.

However, not all Germans saw it this way. Just a few months earlier the war had been going well. The German army had been advancing and victory seemed possible. During the war the Kaiser had not announced any bad news to the German people, so the peace, in November 1918, had come as a shock.

People were now very bitter and were looking for someone to blame. A simple explanation for the defeat quickly spread. The great German army had been 'stabbed in the back' by the new government.

▲ Happy German children riding on a gun carriage as the soldiers come home following the signing of the armistice on 11 November 1918

## THE 'STAB IN THE BACK' MYTH SUMMARISED

> The German army was a great fighting force. Our brave, patriotic soldiers were not defeated on the battlefield. Our army could have won the war. The politicians are to blame. They wanted to stop the war. They caused unrest among civilians and damaged the morale of our troops. They have **stabbed our great country in the back**. This government is full of criminals and the armistice is a disgrace.

Clearly, Germany's defeat in the First World War was not the fault of the leaders of the new Republic. However, this did not matter. Many people in Germany believed that they had been stabbed in the back by the new government. **They blamed the leaders of the Weimar Republic, not the army generals, for Germany's defeat.** As you can see from the poster below, opponents of the Weimar Republic used this to their advantage to weaken support for the leaders of the Weimar Republic.

## Source 1

Wer hat im **Weltkrieg** dem deutschen Heere den Dolchstoß versetzt? Wer ist schuld daran, daß unser Volk und Vaterland so tief ins Unglück sinken mußte? Der Parteisekretär

◀ A German National Party election poster, from 1924. The words at the bottom of the poster say: 'Who stabbed the German armies in the back in the World War? Whose fault is it that our People and Fatherland must sink so deep into misfortune?'

## Discuss

Why might many Germans have wanted to believe in the idea that their soldiers had been 'stabbed in the back' by the leaders of the Weimar Republic?

## PROBLEM 2: THE TREATY OF VERSAILLES

The First World War ended with the signing of the armistice in November 1918. However, it took until June 1919 for the Allies to agree on a peace treaty. The new German government was not invited to the discussions. These discussions took place at Versailles in France so the treaty was called the Treaty of Versailles.

### What did the German people hope for?

The German people hoped for a fair treaty. There were three reasons for this.

**1** The Allies said that they wanted a more democratic Germany. That is what we have created. The Kaiser has gone. **Our new government needs support**, not punishment. The Allies will not punish us for what the Kaiser did.

**2** President Wilson of the USA is on our side. He has already said that the treaty should not be too hard on us. **Wilson has come up with Fourteen Points** that will form the basis of a fair treaty. France and Britain will have to listen to him.

**3** Germany did not start the First World War. **It is not to blame for the war.** All the countries involved should take a share of the blame. We do not expect to be punished for a war we did not start!

## What did the German people get?

The terms of the Treaty of Versailles came as a real shock to the German people. France and Britain put pressure on President Wilson and forced him to accept a treaty that was designed to seriously weaken Germany.

**Discuss**

1   Which parts of the Treaty were most likely to make the German people feel:
    - angry
    - humiliated
    - insecure?
2   Which parts of the Treaty were most likely to cause problems for the Weimar Republic?

### PART 1: LAND
- Germany lost 13 per cent of its land (and about 6 million people living there).
- This lost land had important raw materials, such as coal.
- Germany was split in two. This was to give Poland access to the sea.
- German troops were not allowed in the Rhineland. This was to make the French feel safe from a German attack.
- All Germany's overseas colonies were taken away.

### PART 2: ARMY
- The German army was to be reduced to just 100,000.
- The navy was cut to 15,000 sailors and only six battleships.
- Germany was not allowed submarines, tanks or an air force.

### PART 3: BLAME
- In the 'war guilt' clause, Germany was blamed for the war.
- This enabled the Allies to demand compensation from Germany for all the damage that had been caused.

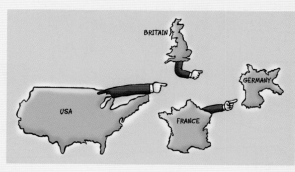

### PART 4: MONEY
- Germany had to pay reparations. Most of the money would go to France and Belgium.
- At Versailles no sum was fixed. But in 1921 the Allies fixed the total amount that Germany had to pay at £6600 million.

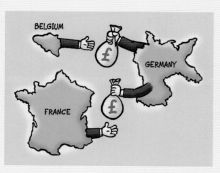

9

## How did the German people react?

The German people felt humiliated by the Treaty of Versailles. They hated the Treaty, and the people who made it.

The German government did not like this Treaty either. However, they had little choice but to accept it. The Allies threatened to restart the war if they did not sign the peace treaty.

However, opponents of the Weimar Republic now blamed the new government for signing the Treaty. To them, the fact that the government had signed the Treaty showed how weak they were and reinforced the view that they had stabbed Germany in the back.

### Source 2

◀ This cartoon appeared in a German newspaper in July 1919. It was called 'Clemenceau the Vampire'. Clemenceau was the leader of France who wanted a treaty that would cripple Germany. The woman on the bed represents Germany

### Source 3

▲ This cartoon appeared in a German magazine, in 1919, attacking the Treaty. The mother is saying to her child: 'When we have paid one hundred billion marks then I can give you something to eat'

### Activity 1

Imagine that you are an editor of a German newspaper in 1919 that is against the government. Design a front page reporting on the Treaty of Versailles. It should include:

- a powerful headline that will sum up the mood of the German people
- a summary of the key points of the Treaty
- a description of how German people feel about the Treaty. Aim to get across the feelings of shock, anger and humiliation
- an explanation of why people feel this way. You could include some quotes from your readers
- a cartoon. You could use one of the cartoons here, or you could research or draw a cartoon of your own
- a comment on why the leaders of the Weimar Republic are to blame for the Treaty.

## PROBLEM 3: POLITICAL VIOLENCE

The Weimar Republic was democratic – people had the right to choose their government. However, some groups did not think that this was the best way to run Germany. These extremist parties wanted to tear the Weimar Republic apart.

### Activity 2

On pages 12–13 you will find details of four extremist groups that used violence to try to overthrow the Weimar Republic. They all harmed the Republic a bit because they reduced the confidence the German people had in their new government. But you must decide which group represented the *biggest threat*.

Your task is to produce a **secret report** for the Weimar government on each of the groups. Your report should:

1 Briefly describe each group and explain how it tried to take over.
2 Examine the strengths and weaknesses of each group. Consider:
   • leadership
   • support
   • organisation
   • how close it came to taking over the country.
3 End by giving each group a danger rating out of 5 (5 = a serious threat; 1 = a small threat). Make sure you explain your rating.

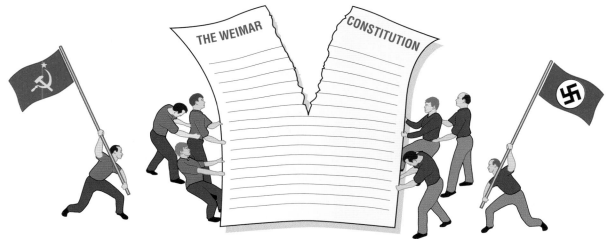

**EXTREME, LEFT-WING PARTIES**
Communist Party
• They believed that they should run the country on behalf of the workers.

**EXTREME, RIGHT-WING PARTIES**
Nazi Party
German National Party
• They believed that Germany should have one strong leader, whom everyone should obey.

## Left-wing violence

# Which extremist political group was the

### THREAT 1: THE SPARTACIST RISING, 1919

**Who?**
The Spartacist League. A Communist group set up by Rosa Luxemburg and Karl Liebknecht.

**Why?**
They did not trust the new government. The Spartacists thought that Ebert would not improve the lives of working people. They wanted a full-scale Communist revolution like the Russian Revolution of 1917.

**What?**
In January 1919 workers were protesting throughout Germany. The Spartacists tried to turn this into a revolution. In Berlin they took over the government's newspaper and telegraph headquarters. They hoped protesters would join them and take over other buildings, but this did not happen. The government ordered the army to stop the uprising. The army was helped by units of the Freikorps. These units were made up of

▲ Spartacists defending the captured newspaper offices

ex-soldiers who were anti-Communist. In the fighting that followed over 100 workers were killed.

**Success?**
The uprising was badly planned. The Spartacists did not get support from other left-wing groups. Rosa Luxemburg was captured by the Freikorps and shot. Her body was dumped in a Berlin canal. Karl Liebknecht was also murdered. Without their main leaders the Spartacists struggled.

### THREAT 2: THE RED RISING IN THE RUHR, 1920

**Who?**
Groups of workers led by members of the Communist Party.

**Why?**
Many German workers were angry about bad pay and bad working conditions. Workers had been protesting throughout 1919.

**What?**
In 1920 a Communist 'Red Army' of 50,000 workers occupied the Ruhr region of Germany and took control of its raw materials. This was one of Germany's main industrial areas. The German army, with the help of the Freikorps, crushed the rising. Over 1000 workers were killed.

▲ The Communist Red Army preparing to fight the Freikorps in 1920

**Success?**
The Communist Party had weak leadership. They did not have a clear plan. Protests did not have widespread, committed support. For the next few years there were lots of demonstrations and strikes, but unrest never seriously threatened the Weimar government's control of Germany.

## Right-wing violence

# biggest threat to the Weimar Republic?

### THREAT 3: THE KAPP PUTSCH, 1920

**Who?**
Freikorps units, led by Wolfgang Kapp.

**Why?**
In 1920 the government ordered that the Freikorps brigades be disbanded. It had little need for them now that left-wing groups had been crushed.

**What?**
Around 12,000 Freikorps marched to Berlin. The government was forced to flee. The Freikorps put forward Kapp as the new leader of Germany.

**Success?**
Kapp and the Freikorps failed to win much support. In Berlin workers went on strike in

▲ Kapp Putsch troops in Berlin

protest at the putsch. This made it impossible for Kapp to rule. After four days he fled from Berlin and Ebert's government returned.

### THREAT 4: THE MUNICH PUTSCH, 1923

**Who?**
The Nazi Party (led by Adolf Hitler) and General Ludendorff (a popular First World War hero who had been involved in the Kapp Putsch). The Nazis had 55,000 members and their own private army called the SA.

**Why?**
Adolf Hitler and the Nazi Party believed that democracy only led to weak government. Instead they thought that there should be one political party, with one leader.

**What?**
The Nazis planned to take over the government and set up General Ludendorff as leader of Germany. They started in Munich. Hitler and 600 of his SA burst into a meeting where the leader of Bavaria (Kahr) was speaking. They forced Kahr to promise to support their plan.

**Success?**
The putsch had not been properly planned. Kahr was allowed to leave the meeting, and the

▲ Putsch leaders pose before their trial. General Ludendorff and Hitler are in the centre

following day he withdrew his support. The German government responded quickly. They ordered the army to crush the revolt. When armed Nazis marched to a military base in Munich they were met by armed police and soldiers. In the fighting that followed fourteen Nazis were killed. The leaders of the putsch were arrested and Hitler was sent to prison for five years. He was released after just nine months, but during this time the Nazis nearly fell apart without their leader.

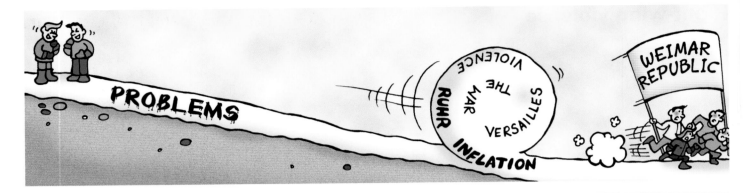

## PROBLEM 4: INVASION OF THE RUHR

Germany struggled to keep up with the reparation payments to the Allies. In 1922 Germany announced that it could not afford to pay reparations for the next three years. France did not believe this and was determined to make Germany pay. In 1923, 60,000 French and Belgian troops marched into the Ruhr, an important industrial area of Germany. They seized control of all mines, factories and railways. They took supplies from shops and set up machine-gun posts in the streets.

## What problems did this cause?

The German government told workers not to co-operate with the French. All workers went on strike. This policy was known as passive resistance. This was meant to be a non-violent protest against the invasion. Despite this, 140 Germans were killed in clashes with troops.

The workers who went on strike received money from the German government, to support their families. This cost the government a lot of money. To make matters worse, no money was coming in from the Ruhr, one of Germany's main industrial areas. The government was running very short of money.

As you can see from the next column, the government's solution to this problem just created an even bigger problem.

**closely linked**

## PROBLEM 5: HYPER-INFLATION

The government becomes very short of money.

**The government prints more money to pay workers and to pay its debts.**

The more money printed, the less it is worth.

People lose confidence in the German mark.

Prices rise at an incredible rate (hyper-inflation).

In January 1919 one US dollar is worth nearly 9 marks.

By November 1923 one dollar is worth 200 billion marks.

At one stage an egg costs 80 million marks and a glass of beer 150 million marks.

By November 1923 the German mark is worthless.

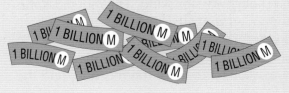

## Source 4

▲ German children, in 1923, show how many German marks are equal to one US dollar

# How did hyper-inflation affect the German people?

Hyper-inflation affected people in different ways, as you can see from the table below. However, there were far more losers than winners. For most people in Germany in 1923, life became very difficult.

| HYPER-INFLATION | |
| --- | --- |
| **Winners** | **Losers** |
| People in debt found it easier to pay off their loans. | People with savings were the biggest losers. The value of what they had saved fell drastically.<br>Pensioners were badly hit. In 1919, 6000 marks was a small fortune. By 1923 it would not even buy a stamp for a letter! |
| Businessmen found it easier to pay back money they had borrowed to build up their businesses. | Workers found that wage increases did not keep up with rising prices. |

There were major food shortages because farmers did not want to sell food for worthless money. There were deaths from starvation. Some people turned to crime because life was so hard.

Source 6 shows how everyday life was affected.

## Source 5

▲ A woman using banknotes to start her fire, 1923

## Source 6

An account written by someone who lived through hyper-inflation in Germany:

On Friday afternoons in 1923, very long lines of workers waited outside the pay windows of the big German factories … until at last they reached the pay window and received a bag full of paper banknotes.

The figures on the banknotes could be as high as 18 trillion marks.

As soon as they got their money the workers began running to food stores. Here there were slow queues. If you got there first a half kilo of sugar could be bought for 2 million marks. If you were at the back of the queue, by the time you got to the counter, 2 million marks would only buy you a quarter of a kilo of sugar.

People carried their money around in sacks or prams. Life was madness, nightmare, desperation and chaos.

# Did hyper-inflation damage the Weimar Republic more than any other problem?

The Weimar Republic was seriously weakened by hyper-inflation. Millions lost their savings and there was widespread poverty. As we have seen, ordinary, respectable Germans, who had worked hard all their lives, lost out, whilst debtors and big business did well. This turned many people against the government.

It was hard to have confidence in the government when everything was in such chaos. Some of the government's other problems had been outside their control but hyper-inflation was caused by the government's own actions. This made many moderate people turn against the Weimar Republic.

In future years few people in Germany would forget the damage caused by hyper-inflation. Some historians have claimed that it damaged the Weimar Republic more than any other event in the first five years of its existence. What do you think?

## Activity

Look at the five problems the Weimar Republic faced between 1918 and 1923:

- **DEFEAT IN THE FIRST WORLD WAR – THE 'STAB IN THE BACK'**

- **THE TREATY OF VERSAILLES**

- **POLITICAL VIOLENCE**

- **INVASION OF THE RUHR**

- **HYPER-INFLATION**

Rank these in order, starting with the problem that you think damaged the Weimar Republic the most, and ending with the one that you think damaged it the least. Explain each decision you make.

# How were the problems faced by the Weimar Republic linked together?

## Activity

Look at the picture below. Five students are working together to find links between the different problems faced by the Weimar Republic. One link has been explained for you.

1 On your own version of this diagram, in bubble 2 explain how the Treaty of Versailles is linked to Political Violence. In bubble 3 explain how the Treaty is linked to the Invasion of the Ruhr.

2 Can you find any other links between other problems? Make sure that you can explain the links.

3 Which problem do you think was at the root of the difficulties facing the Weimar Republic? Look for the problem that is linked to the most other problems.

## Concept maps

Being able to understand the problems faced by the Weimar Republic and how they were linked together is an important part of this Enquiry in Depth. As you will see on page 18, exam questions often focus on this part of the course. Building a concept map with other students is a good way of revising this key topic. Concept maps help you to:

- develop good explanations
- identify the key factors that explain an event or development (in this case why the Weimar Republic faced problems)
- show how the factors worked together
- show which factors were the most important.

By now you should feel like an expert on the Weimar Republic in the early 1920s! However, simply knowing a lot is not enough to achieve a good grade in the GCSE exam. These Meet the Examiner features are here to help you turn all that knowledge into an excellent answer.

The examiners are not trying to catch you out: they are giving you a chance to show what you know – **and what you can do with what you know**. If you work out what the question is getting at, you will be able to answer it from what you have learned.

To stay relevant to the questions you will need to practise how to '**decode**' questions.

**Step 1:** Read the question a couple of times.
**Step 2:** Highlight each of the following. You could use a different colour for each.

**Date boundaries** – What time period should you cover in your answer? Stick to this carefully otherwise you waste time writing about events that are not relevant to the question.

**Content focus** – The topic the examiner wants you to focus on.

**Question type** – Different question types require different approaches. Look for key words, like '**Why**', '**How important**' or '**How did**', that will help you work out what type of approach is needed.

**Marks available** – Look at how many marks the question is worth. This gives you a guide as to how much you are expected to write. Do not spend too long on questions that are only worth a few marks.

Look at the exam question below.

▲ This cartoon appeared in a German magazine, in 1919, attacking the Treaty. The mother is saying to her child: 'When we have paid one hundred billion marks then I can give you something to eat'

The content focus for this question is the **Treaty of Versailles** and how it caused problems for the Weimar Republic.

The question asks you to **explain why** the Treaty of Versailles caused problems. You need to do more than simply describe the key terms of the treaty. You need to show how these key terms led to major problems for the Republic.

> Using Source A and your own knowledge explain why the Treaty of Versailles caused problems for the Weimar Republic in the early 1920s. [8]

You must stick to the date boundaries of the question. In this case **the early 1920s**. Details of how the Treaty of Versailles led to problems in the late 1920s will not gain you extra marks.

**8 marks** are available. This indicates that a developed answer is required. You will need more than a short paragraph or a quick list of key points.

# Meet the Examiner: Using a source and your own knowledge to write effective explanations

## Five top tips:

### 1. Use the source

In exam questions such as this the source should help you get started. In this case Source A suggests that the reparations that Germany had to pay as a result of the Treaty of Versailles led to economic problems and caused German families great hardship.

### 2. Use your own knowledge but be selective

Just using the source will not be enough to get you a high mark for this question. Use your own knowledge to explain how the Treaty of Versailles led to other problems. However, do not list all the terms of the Treaty. Be selective – choose the terms that led to major problems for the Republic.

### 3. Give a range of examples

Make sure that you do not focus on just one problem caused by the Treaty. Try and give a range of examples that show how the Treaty caused problems for the Weimar Republic.

### 4. Tie what you know to the question

Do not 'say' that a term from the Treaty of Versailles caused a problem; **prove it!**

Explain how the term caused a problem. You can do this by using connectives such as:

> 'This led to ...'
> 'This meant that ...'
> 'This resulted in ...'

### 5. Plan your answer

Make sure your answer is well organised. It is important that you quickly plan your answer before you start to write it. Use paragraphs! In this case each paragraph could deal with a problem caused by the Treaty.

### Activity

1 Use the Meet the Examiner advice to answer the exam question on page 18.
2 Swap your answer with a partner. Use the five top tips to evaluate their answer. Have they followed all five tips? Highlight sections of their answer that show that they have followed the advice provided by the examiner.

For your GCSE you need to develop your recall skills. It is no good going into the exam knowing how to structure a good answer if you cannot remember any important information in the first place! How do you normally revise? You probably make revision notes or simply read through your folder. Throughout this book you will be provided with some different strategies to try out. Experiment and find out which method works best for you.

SMARTER REVISION can save you time and improve your grades!

## TIP 1: Acronyms

### How can a lamb help you to remember the terms of the Treaty of Versailles?

Revision does not have to be boring! Inventing your own acronyms can help you remember key pieces of information. The odder they are the more likely you are to remember them.

Take, for example, the Treaty of Versailles. You need to remember the four key terms of the Treaty. Think of the Germans being like LAMBS to the slaughter. A LAMB can help you to remember the key terms.

**L** = **Land** (Germany lost 13 per cent of its land.)

**A** = **Army** (The German army was cut to just 100,000.)

**M** = **Money** (Germany was made to pay reparations.)

**B** = **Blame** (Germany was blamed for starting the war.)

## TIP 2: Memory maps

### How can a map save you time and boost your memory?

- Memory maps encourage you to link pieces of information together. You learn more by making links, because it makes you think! You are actively involved with your revision. This is a lot better than simply reading through your folder hoping that your brain will act as a sponge and soak up the information!

- Memory maps can save you time – you do not need to write everything down. Do not write full sentences. Be ruthless! **Use key words or phrases**. This makes it easier to build up branches without using the whole page. You can't write down everything you know about a topic, and you don't need to! Ninety per cent of the words that students write down when they make revision notes are not needed for recall purposes!

- Lots of you will find it easier to remember visual images than words. You may remember more if you add your own pictures, cartoons or images. **Use pictures/images/diagrams** as often as you can, to replace words or to emphasise words.

- You can **include acronyms**. Remember the odder the better!

- Memory maps can be added to over time and built up over a module or unit of work. Add to or *redraft* your map when you do later work that revisits or builds on the ideas in the map. So remember to **leave some space**!

- Finally, and perhaps most importantly, memory maps make revision a lot more interesting! They are also a flexible tool for revision. You can produce a memory map from memory, check it against the original, then add in what you have missed.

# How to build a memory map

**Step 1** Use plain A4 or, even better, A3 paper (landscape). Space is important. The end result should not look too busy or cramped.

**Step 2** Draw the first draft of your map in pencil so that you can make any corrections that are needed.

**Step 3** Draw a central picture which sums up the topic for you. Start in the middle … then build out …

**Step 4** Divide the topic into sub-topics – what are the main ideas in the topic? Work in a clockwise direction (starting at 12 o'clock). Draw a line out from the central image (this is like a large **bough** of a tree) for each theme/sub-topic. Write the theme/sub-topic on the bough. If possible, each theme should be in a different colour.

**Step 5** Draw **branches** off the main bough using the same colour. On each branch write down key words connected to the theme or sub-topic. Write these slightly smaller than the main theme.

**Step 6** You can now sub-divide again. Draw thinner lines off the branches (**twigs** if you like) to record any ideas that are connected to the words on each branch. You can continue sub-dividing, depending on the amount of detail you wish to include. As you move further away from the centre, the ideas become less important (central) to the main topic. This is reflected by decreasing the size of the words and images as you move away from the centre.

## Activity

Use the advice on pages 20–21 to complete your own version of the memory map below. You can use your own images if you wish.

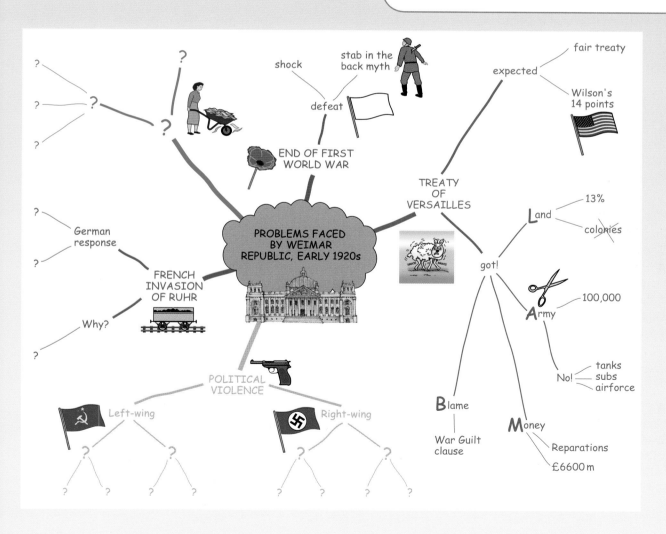

# 1.2 Was the Weimar Republic ever a success?

The story of the Weimar Republic is not all doom and gloom. For five 'Golden Years', 1924–1929, things appeared to go well in Germany. But you must judge for yourself if the old problems had really been dealt with, or just papered over.

## Problems faced by the Weimar Republic in 1923

**POLICY A**
Print even more money. Use it to pay the workers on strike in the Ruhr and to pay compensation to people who have lost their savings.

**PROBLEM 1**
Hyper-inflation

**POLICY B**
Scrap the old money system and set up a new currency.

**POLICY A**
Call off passive resistance. Promise to begin paying reparations again to France to persuade them to leave.

**PROBLEM 2**
French occupation of the Ruhr

**POLICY B**
Continue passive resistance. Pay the workers in the Ruhr so that they can continue their strike. Threaten to force the French to leave if they won't go willingly.

**POLICY A**
Threaten war unless you are given back the land you lost in the Treaty of Versailles. Secretly start building up your army.

**PROBLEM 3**
Germany is not trusted by other countries

**POLICY B**
Make a series of treaties with other European countries. Promise to stick to the terms of the Treaty of Versailles and not to try to regain the land you lost.

**POLICY A**
Refuse to pay the Allies any more money. Argue that the terms of the Treaty of Versailles are unfair and that it is impossible to keep up with reparation payments.

**PROBLEM 4**
Germany is facing massive reparations

**POLICY B**
Promise to stick to the terms of the Treaty and pay reparations in full. Try and persuade the Allies to let you have longer to pay back the money you owe. Borrow money from the rich USA so that you can start paying back reparations immediately.

**POLICY A**
Try to get loans from the rich USA. Use this money to build new homes, roads and hospitals. Tax rich people more and use the money to increase pensions and help the unemployed.

**PROBLEM 5**
Germany needs to rebuild its economy

**POLICY B**
Refuse to ask for foreign loans. Argue that it is humiliating and that Germany should not be dependent on other countries. Provide jobs for the unemployed by building up the army. Instead of paying reparations use the money to build homes and roads.

# To what extent did Stresemann solve the problems facing the Weimar Republic?

In August 1923 Gustav Stresemann became Chancellor of Germany. The problems he faced were so great most Germans did not think that he or any of the politicians of the Weimar Republic would be able to solve them.

For the next five years (first as Chancellor, then as Foreign Minister) Stresemann tried to find answers to the problems facing the Weimar Republic. How far he succeeded is a debate among historians. It is time for you to join the debate!

**Activity**

**What would you have done?**

Look carefully at the problems and possible policies facing Germany in 1923 (page 22). Which policy do you think would be best to deal with each problem? Explain your decisions.

**HISTORIAN A SAYS:** 'Stresemann – the man who built a strong Germany'

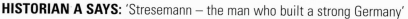

Stresemann was one of Germany's greatest leaders. He came up with clever solutions to the problems that Germany faced in 1923 and built a strong Germany. By the time he died in 1929, Germany had one of the strongest economies in Europe. It was trusted and well respected by other countries. So the period 1924–1929 is rightly called the 'Golden Twenties'.

**HISTORIAN B SAYS:** 'Stresemann – the man who papered over the cracks'

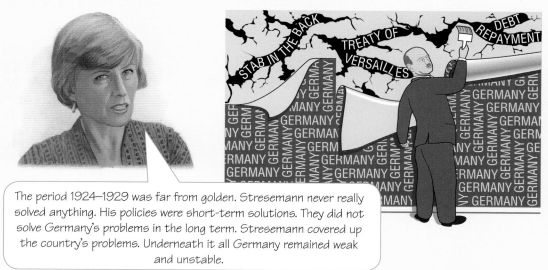

The period 1924–1929 was far from golden. Stresemann never really solved anything. His policies were short-term solutions. They did not solve Germany's problems in the long term. Stresemann covered up the country's problems. Underneath it all Germany remained weak and unstable.

### Activity

1 Use pages 24–25 to fill in your own copy of the table below. In the last column give Stresemann a star rating to show how successful each policy was. (***** = brilliant solution; * = very poor solution.)

| Problem | Stresemann's policy | Positive results | Negative results | Star rating |
|---|---|---|---|---|
| Hyper-inflation | | | | |
| French occupation of the Ruhr | | | | |
| Germany is not trusted by other countries | | | | |
| Germany is facing massive reparations | | | | |
| Germany needs to rebuild its economy | | | | |

2 Look for similarities and differences between what Stresemann did and what policies you chose for the activity on page 23. Do you think that Stresemann made mistakes, or did he have no other option?

## Stresemann's solutions

### POLICY 1: Introduce a new currency

- Stresemann acted quickly to deal with hyper-inflation. The old money was replaced with a new currency called the Rentenmark. One Rentenmark replaced 1000 billion marks. Old notes were recalled and burned.

**Result ...**
- The new currency was quickly accepted by the German people. Inflation was brought under control.

**However ...**
- The German people never forgot hyper-inflation. People who had lost their savings were not compensated. They felt cheated and they blamed the Weimar Republic.

### POLICY 2: Persuade the French to leave the Ruhr

- Stresemann called off passive resistance, because it had not forced the French to withdraw from the Ruhr and it had created serious economic problems.
- He promised to keep up reparation payments to France.

**Result ...**
- The French left the Ruhr.

**However ...**
- This was a very unpopular policy in Germany. There was a lot of opposition to it, especially from right-wing extremists. They claimed that it was a sign of weak government: Stresemann had 'given in' to the French.

## POLICY 3: Improve Germany's relationship with other countries

- Stresemann decided to co-operate with other countries in Europe. He accepted that Germany could not reclaim the land it had lost in the Treaty of Versailles. He hoped that by doing so the Allies would change the terms of the Treaty.

**Result ...**

- In 1925 Stresemann signed the Locarno Pact. This was a series of treaties with Britain, France, Belgium and Italy in which they promised not to invade one another.
- In 1926 Germany joined the League of Nations. It was given great power status which meant that it could have a say in major decisions that had to be made.
- In 1926 Stresemann was awarded the Nobel Peace Prize.

**However ...**

- Some Germans thought that Stresemann was weak. By saying that Germany would not try to regain the land it had lost he had once again 'given in' to France.
- Some army generals believed that Stresemann should have built up the army instead, and tried to regain the land lost in the Treaty of Versailles by force.

## POLICY 4: Continue to pay reparations

- Stresemann realised that he could not force the Allies to change the Treaty so he promised to pay reparations. He hoped that the Allies would lower the payments in the future.

**Result ...**

- The Dawes Plan of 1924 reorganised the way that Germans had to pay reparations. Germany was given a longer period to pay the Allies.
- In 1929 the Young Plan lowered the amount of money Germany had to pay in reparations from 132,000 million marks to 37,000 million.

**However ...**

- The Dawes Plan did not reduce the amount of money Germany had to pay in reparations. Opponents of the Weimar Republic called the Dawes Plan 'a second Versailles'.
- The Young Plan was also hated by many Germans who thought that Germany should not have to pay reparations at all. Under the terms of the Young Plan, Germany would be paying reparations until 1988.

## POLICY 5: Get help to rebuild the economy

- Stresemann organised big loans for Germany from the USA. This was part of the Dawes Plan (1924).

**Result ...**

- The German government used this money to improve housing, hospitals, schools and roads.
- Loans were also given to private German firms.
- In addition, many US firms set up factories in Germany.
- Pensions and wages rose (for some).

**However ...**

- The German economy was now very dependent on the US economy. Problems in the USA would cause massive problems in Germany. Even Stresemann himself admitted that Germany was 'dancing on a volcano'.
- Wages did not rise for everyone. Farmers lost out because food prices stayed low. By 1929 farmworkers earned only half the national average wage. Many farmers became angry and started to support extreme groups, such as the Nazis, who offered to help them.
- Unemployment never fell below 1 million. From 1928 it started to rise even higher.
- Rich people in Germany had to pay higher taxes. They complained that the government was spending too much money on helping the poor and the unemployed.

### And one more thing ...

After 1923 Germany became more peaceful. There was less political violence. Between 1924 and 1928 there were no attempts to overthrow the Weimar Republic.

# Meet the Examiner: Using visual sources

GCSE History is not all about writing essays. You also need to be able to use written and visual sources effectively. Here is a sample exam question. This type of question is often known as an **inference question**. It is usually the first question on the exam paper.

**Activity**

1  Use the advice below to help you finish annotating Sources A and B.
2  When you have finished, attempt the sample exam question.

What do Sources A and B suggest about the role that Stresemann played in leading the Weimar Republic?　　　[4]

## Advice

When you are using sources for a historical enquiry it is always a good idea to annotate the sources. Written sources and visual sources such as cartoons often contain a very strong message. Try to work out, or infer, what the message is by following the steps below.

**Step 1: Identify the clues** in the source that can help you answer the question.

Look at Source A. A lot of time and thought goes into designing cartoons and posters. Look at the key features of the source. Annotate the people and objects in the source.

**Step 2: Develop inferences**

Ask yourself the key questions: Why has the artist included these details? What do these clues suggest about Stresemann's role?

• Why is Germany walking on a tightrope?
• Why is Germany crossing a ravine?
• Why are there flowers on the other side?
• Why is Stresemann an angel?

## WARNING!

Inference questions are usually only worth four marks so you should not spend too long on these questions. One paragraph should be enough for full marks.

The key things to remember are:

• **Stick to the focus of the question:** stick to what you can learn from the source. There is no need to evaluate how trustworthy the source is. You will waste valuable time and pick up no extra marks.

• **Support the inferences you make with references to the source:** it is better to make two supported inferences than it is to make five or six inferences that you do not back up by referring to details in the source.

• **Use both sources:** if the question asks you to use two sources, use two! If you comment on only one you will lose marks.

## INFERENCES: What does the source suggest?

### CLUES: What does the source tell us?

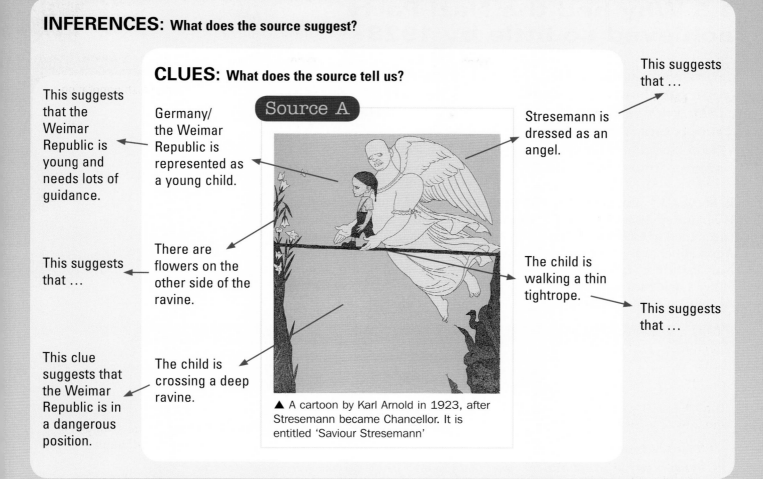

This suggests that the Weimar Republic is young and needs lots of guidance.

Germany/ the Weimar Republic is represented as a young child.

This suggests that ...

There are flowers on the other side of the ravine.

This clue suggests that the Weimar Republic is in a dangerous position.

The child is crossing a deep ravine.

This suggests that ...

Stresemann is dressed as an angel.

The child is walking a thin tightrope.

This suggests that ...

▲ A cartoon by Karl Arnold in 1923, after Stresemann became Chancellor. It is entitled 'Saviour Stresemann'

## INFERENCES: What does the source suggest?

This suggests that Stresemann's policies had been successful.

### CLUES: What does the source tell us?

The source tells us that the Weimar Republic was much stronger after 1924.

**Source B**

F Reynoldson, *Weimar and Nazi Germany*, published in 1996:

From 1924 to 1929 the Weimar Republic was much stronger than it had been just after the war. Led by Stresemann in the Reichstag, the different parties managed to work together. The extreme parties gained fewer seats in the elections. The German people were better off and more contented. The Weimar Republic looked safe.

The source tells us that extreme parties did not do very well in the elections.

This suggests that ...

# 1.3 Why had the Nazi Party achieved so little by 1928?

> Now we must go back to the end of the First World War to find out about Hitler and the Nazis. You will find out what they were saying and doing, and how they gained supporters. You must explain who was attracted to the Nazi message and why support for the Party did not amount to much by 1928.

In Section 1.1 you investigated four groups that tried to overthrow the Weimar Republic. One of these groups was the Nazi Party. In 1923 the Nazis tried to take over Germany by force. They failed, and their leader, Adolf Hitler, was sent to prison. However, this was not the end of the Nazi Party, nor was it the last the German people would hear of Adolf Hitler. Look back to the report that you wrote on the Nazi party for the Activity on page 11. It will help you with your next big task.

## Activity

*December, 1928*

*Dear Secret Agent*

*We were very impressed with the report that you wrote for the German government about the different groups that planned to overthrow the Weimar Republic. We would like to use your expertise again.*

*We are still interested in the activities of the Nazi Party. Since his release from prison, its leader, Adolf Hitler, has been working very hard to rebuild the Nazi Party. Your task is to find out as much as you can about Hitler, the Nazi Party and its supporters. What do they really stand for? Are they well organised? Are they more dangerous now than they were in 1923?*

*This time we would like you to present your findings to us in person. All the leading members of the government will be present, so you need to plan your presentation carefully. We have put together four Evidence Files to help you with your research (see pages 29–32). We suggest that you organise your presentation under the following headings:*

***Section 1: Leadership*** *– Who is Adolf Hitler? What is his background? Is he an effective leader?*

***Section 2: Beliefs*** *– What does the Nazi Party stand for? What are its big ideas?*

***Section 3: Organisation*** *– Is the Nazi Party well organised?*

***Section 4: Support*** *– Who supports the Nazi Party? How much support does it have?*

***Section 5: Danger rating*** *– Do you think that the Nazi Party has grown more dangerous since 1923?*

*(Use a danger rating scale: !!!!! = very dangerous; ! = no threat at all. Does it look as if they will get into power soon?)*

# FILE 1: LEADER PROFILE – ADOLF HITLER

## Early life

- Born in 1889 in Austria.
- Unhappy at school. He is moody, shy and lonely.
- Poor at most subjects (except gym and art).
- 1903 – Father dies.
- Leaves school with no qualifications.

## Life after school

- 1907 – Mother dies. Goes to Vienna. Fails to gain a place at Academy of Fine Arts. Struggles to make money and lives almost as a down-and-out.
- 1914 – Joins the German army. Fights in the First World War, winning a medal for bravery.
- 1918 – Angry to hear of Germany's surrender. Feels betrayed.

## Political life

- 1919 – Employed as a spy by the army. Sent to a meeting of the German Workers' Party. Finds himself agreeing with many of their ideas. Joins as their 55th member.
- 1920 – Helps to write their political programme (**see File 2**). The Party is renamed the National Socialist German Workers' Party (or Nazi Party).
- 1921 – Hitler becomes leader of the Nazi Party. He sets up the SA (**see File 3**), the Nazi Party's private army.
- Support for the Nazi Party grows. By the end of 1922 it has 20,000 members.
- 1923 – The Munich Putsch. The Nazis attempt to overthrow the government by force. The putsch fails but the trial and publicity that follow give Hitler the chance to make a name for himself.
- 1924 – In prison, he writes *Mein Kampf* (My Struggle). This book outlines his main ideas about how Germany should be ruled (**see File 2**). Hitler is released from prison early. He starts to rebuild the Nazi Party, improving the way it is organised and changing its tactics (**see File 3**). His aim now is to use democratic means, rather than force, to get into power.

## Leadership qualities

- Tremendous energy.
- Charismatic and inspirational.
- Single-minded and suspicious of others.
- Great public speaker. His timing, the style of his delivery and the content of his speeches captivates his listeners.

# FILE 2: BELIEFS

## The Programme (aims) of the National Socialist German Workers' Party, 1920

- Destroy the Treaty of Versailles and end reparations.
- Only those of German blood may be members of the nation (Germany). Therefore no Jew may be a member of the nation.
- All non-German immigration to be stopped.
- Take over land in Eastern Europe in order to provide 'living space' for the growing German population.
- Criminals against the nation should be punished by death.
- Provide generous old age pensions.
- Abolish incomes not earned by work.
- Help should be given to small businesses.
- Change the education system. Pupils should be taught to love their country. Physical fitness should be encouraged. Sport and gymnastics must be compulsory.

FILE 2

## Extracts from *Mein Kampf*, 1924

One strong leader. Debate and discussion produce weak government. There should be no majority decisions. Instead of democracy, decisions should be taken by one man.

Smash Communism.

The Aryans (white Europeans) are the Master Race. All other races (especially the Jews) are inferior.

Unite all Germans in one country.

Rebuild the army and invade land in Eastern Europe. Armed struggle is an essential part of life.

# FILE 3: ORGANISATION AND TACTICS

## Report on Nazi Party tactics, 1928

The Nazis appear to have changed their tactics. Hitler seems to have realised that they cannot seize power by force. He is trying to build up support for the Nazi Party so that it can take power by democratic means. Since Hitler's release from prison he has reorganised the Nazi Party to make it more electable.

- The Nazis have been running **evening classes** for their members in order to make them better public speakers.
- Local leaders of the Nazi Party have been organising **public meetings**, with visiting speakers, in an attempt to gain more supporters.
- The Nazis receive most of their **money** from ordinary members, through donations and charges to attend meetings.
- Their **propaganda** is very effective and they concentrate on issues that people think are important.
- They have adopted the raised right arm as a salute and the **swastika** as their symbol. Hitler himself has designed their flag.

## Report on the SA, 1928

SA stands for 'Sturm-Abteilung', or Stormtroopers. The SA are sometimes known as 'Brownshirts' because of the colour of their uniform. More than half of the members come from the unemployed and many are ex-soldiers who fought in the First World War. The SA provide them with food and sometimes a home in SA-run hostels.

The SA are growing increasingly powerful. Hitler set up the SA in 1921 to stop Nazi meetings being interrupted by followers of other parties. However, now the SA are far more likely to disrupt the meetings of their opponents. Hitler uses them like a bunch of hired thugs. Their aim is to use any means possible to stop opponents of the Nazi Party spreading their message. Hitler has said, 'We must struggle with ideas, but if necessary also with fists.'

The SA are very important to Hitler. They protect Nazi speakers and help to deliver propaganda leaflets to peoples' homes. Some Germans are put off by their violence but others seem to be impressed by their organisation.

F
I
L
E

3

# FILE 4: SUPPORT

## Report on the 1928 election

The Nazis must be very disappointed with the result of the 1928 election. The great majority of workers supported the Social Democrats. With the help of foreign loans, Stresemann has got the economy back on track. Many factory workers feel that they are doing quite well at the moment. Those workers who do want major changes seem to be voting for the Communist Party. In the last election the Communists gained four times as many votes as the Nazis. Hitler does not appear to be getting his message across to workers.

The Nazis have been more successful with farmers and the owners of small businesses. These groups have not done so well recently and are starting to turn to the Nazis.

More people than ever before are members of the Nazi Party. Membership has almost doubled between 1923 and 1928. However, the vast majority of Germans do not appear to be attracted to the Nazi Party. After all, the Nazis got under 3 per cent of the overall votes in the election.

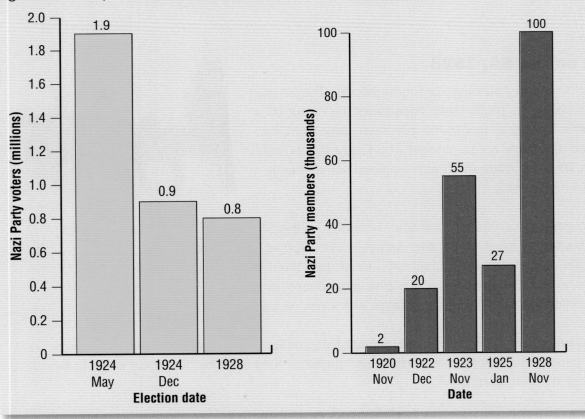

F
I
L
E

4

# Who did the Nazis appeal to in 1928?

**Dietrich**

I was proud to fight for Germany in the First World War. The army was stabbed in the back by the criminals who signed the peace treaty. I loved army life – the uniform, the friendship, the excitement. During the war my life had a purpose. Now I just work in a factory. This country needs strong leadership, like we had in the army. With a strong leader our country could become great again.

**Josef**

I'm a Jewish businessman. I also fought for Germany in the First World War. The Treaty of Versailles was a disgrace. Our government should never have given in to the Allies. During the early 1920s I lost a lot of my savings because of hyper-inflation. However, Stresemann seems to have sorted things out and my business is doing well. I hope it continues.

**Maria**

I am a 20-year-old student and an active member of the Communist Party. I think the government should be doing more to help the workers. All the money goes to the handful of rich industrialists who own the factories. Things need to change.

**Franz**

**Helga**

My husband's factory is doing very well at the moment. Stresemann has done a great job. The US loans have been a real boost. Business is booming. I'm also pleased that all the political violence has stopped. There is no place for violence in a civilised country. The only thing that scares me is the Communists. It would be a disaster if they took over the country. The last thing we want is for Germany to go the same way as the Soviet Union.

I am a farm worker. The farmer I work for has had to cut my wages. I don't blame him, I blame the government. Farmers are losing out because of low food prices and the politicians don't seem to care. I'm also worried about my parents. They are both pensioners. They lost a lot of money during the hyper-inflation a few years ago. They have worked hard all their lives but they are struggling to survive on what they receive from the government.

# 1.4 How did Hitler become Chancellor in 1933?

In 1928 few Germans would have predicted that Hitler would become leader of Germany. The Nazi Party did not appear to be going anywhere. Yet by July 1932 the Nazis were the most popular party, and in January 1933 Hitler became Chancellor. You need to identify the key reasons behind Hitler's dramatic rise to power.

In this section two teams of historians are going to try to persuade you that they have the strongest explanation. You need to think carefully and make your own decision. **Which team of historians are you going to support in the tug-of-war?**

**Activity**

**Step 1 – Evidence collection**
On pages 36–41 each team member puts forward an argument to support their team's overall case. Record their argument and any evidence that they use to support it. You could use a memory map or a table to help you record your findings.

**Step 2 – Weigh the evidence that you have collected**
How strong is the argument put forward by each team member? Give each team member a rating out of 10 to show how important you think their argument is.
Then ask yourself the key question – which team do you think has the strongest overall argument?

**Step 3 – Present your case**
Write a speech supporting the team you think has the strongest argument. Aim to use written sources, graphs, statistics and photographs to support your case.

Be prepared to take part in a debate with the rest of your class. You may find that some of them disagree with you!

My team disagree! We believe that the Nazis were helped by **events they had no control over**. The Wall Street Crash, fear of Communism, weak opponents and a political deal are the key factors that explain how Hitler got into power.

# OTHER EVENTS

I believe that the key event in Hitler's rise to power was the **Wall Street Crash**. This led to a terrible economic crisis in Germany. This crisis was known as the Great Depression and it explains why many people started to vote for extreme parties like the Nazis.

## THE WALL STREET CRASH

**Why did events in the USA cause problems in Germany?**

When the US stockmarket on Wall Street crashed, in 1929, it created many problems. People lost the confidence to invest in companies and US banks and businesses lost large sums of money. As a result, one in four people became unemployed.

This created serious problems for countries in Europe that traded with the USA. Germany was particularly badly hit. The whole German economy was very dependent on loans from America. As can be seen in the diagram below, a vicious circle was created causing unemployment and widespread poverty. This period in German history is known as the Great Depression.

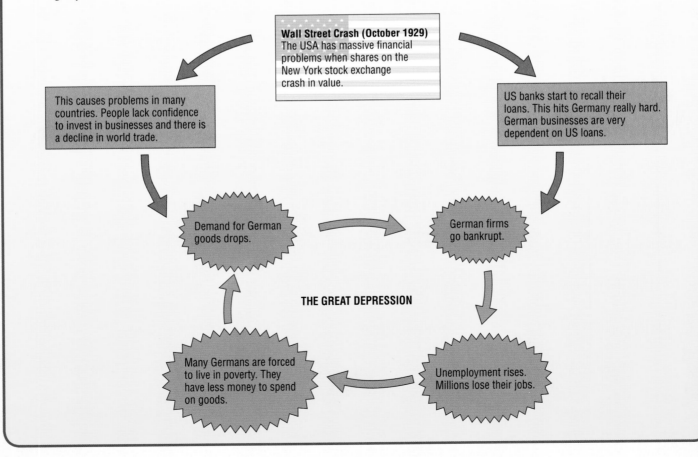

**Wall Street Crash (October 1929)**
The USA has massive financial problems when shares on the New York stock exchange crash in value.

This causes problems in many countries. People lack confidence to invest in businesses and there is a decline in world trade.

US banks start to recall their loans. This hits Germany really hard. German businesses are very dependent on US loans.

Demand for German goods drops.

German firms go bankrupt.

**THE GREAT DEPRESSION**

Many Germans are forced to live in poverty. They have less money to spend on goods.

Unemployment rises. Millions lose their jobs.

The Great Depression had three main effects.

**1 The Depression made life a great struggle for people**

Many businesses went bankrupt. Those that survived saw their profits drop. Farmers also struggled and many went out of business. By 1932 unemployment had reached 6 million.

**2 The Depression made the Weimar government look weak**

The politicians could not agree what to do to help poor people and the unemployed. As so many people had lost their jobs, the government received less money from taxes. They did not want to spend extra money that they did not have to help the poor because they thought that it could lead to hyper-inflation (as it had done in 1923). So, to start with, they did nothing. Then, when they did act, they actually cut back on the money they spent. This made the government unpopular.

## THIS LED TO ...

**3 The Depression increased support for extreme parties**

The Great Depression made people angry. Many blamed the political parties that had been running the country and the democratic way that the Weimar Republic was governed. People started to support more extreme political parties, such as the Nazis, instead.

These graphs show that as unemployment increased so did the votes for more extreme political parties.

### Source 1

▼ Unemployment figures and votes for the Nazis and the Communists in Reichstag elections, 1928–1932

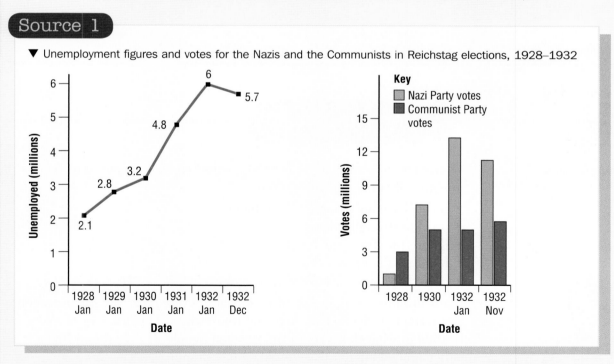

# OWN ACTIONS

Hold on! It's about time you heard from some of my team. We admit that events such as the Wall Street Crash helped the Nazis but we do not believe that this is the main reason that they were able to get into power. If you really want to understand how Hitler got into power you need to look at what the Nazis were doing *themselves*. Here are **four key actions** they took.

## A   HITLER'S LEADERSHIP SKILLS

**Hitler's leadership skills** played a crucial role in the Nazis' rise to power. His speeches and personality gained the Nazis a great deal of support. He came across as a strong leader who could solve Germany's problems.

Hitler was a strong leader who was able to make people believe that he alone could save them from the problems facing Germany. He was also a very charismatic and powerful public speaker. He seemed to be able to identify with his audience and to fill them with a sense of hope.

### Source 2

Adapted from *Darkness over Germany*, 1943, by E. A. Buller:

As Hitler spoke I was most interested to hear the reactions of the men around me. 'He speaks for me, he speaks for me.' 'Oh God, he knows how I feel.' Many of them seemed lost to the world around them and were probably unaware of what they were saying. One man in particular struck me as he lent forward with his head in his hands, and with a sort of sob said, 'God be thanked, he understands.'

## B   NAZI PROMISES

**Nazi promises.**
The Nazis said what people wanted to hear. They made sure that their promises were flexible and contained something for everyone. This explains why they were so well supported.

The Nazis concentrated on issues that the German people were very unhappy about. They promised to:

- solve Germany's economic problems
- provide strong leadership
- ignore the Treaty of Versailles
- build up the army
- make Germany a great country again.

Their promises were designed to appeal to everyone, from businessmen and farmers to factory workers and housewives. The Nazis were also flexible in what they said to the German people. If they found that a policy was unpopular they would simply drop it.

## C   ORGANISATION

*Organisation.* The Nazis were also very well organised. This impressed voters and helped the Nazis to campaign more effectively than their main rivals.

- The Nazis were good at raising money for their election campaigns. A lot of this money came from ordinary members. The Nazis were also able to attract huge donations from rich businessmen like Fritz Thyssen.
- Nazi Party members worked hard in their local regions to spread the Nazi message through door-to-door leafleting and public meetings. The Nazis also organised soup kitchens and shelter for the unemployed.
- The SA also played an important role. With their uniforms and marches the SA looked capable of bringing law and order to Germany.

### Source 3

*Inside the Third Reich* by Albert Speer:

… during these months my mother saw an SA parade in the streets. The sight of discipline in a time of chaos, the impression of energy in a time of hopelessness, seems to have won her over. Without ever having heard a speech or read a pamphlet, she joined the party.

## D   NAZI PROPAGANDA

*Nazi propaganda* was the main reason why support for the Nazis grew. It presented the Nazi Party as the solution to Germany's problems.

Nazi propaganda was organised by Josef Goebbels. The Nazis used the latest technology – loudspeakers, slide shows and films – to spread their message.

The Nazis used mass rallies and marches to give the impression of discipline and order. They also used powerful propaganda posters with simple slogans, like the one shown here, to spread their key ideas.

### Source 4

▼ 'Our last hope: Hitler'. A Nazi election poster from 1932

# OTHER EVENTS

The opposing team have put forward some important points, but there is more to our case than just the Wall Street Crash. We feel that **three** other **important factors** helped the Nazis get into power.

## A

## FEAR OF COMMUNISM

**Fear of Communism.** I believe that the Nazis were very lucky to receive so much support. Many people voted for them because they were scared of the Communists getting into power. The Nazis seemed to be the only party who could stop the Communists.

From 1930 to 1932 support for the Communists increased. The German Communist Party was the largest in Europe, outside the Soviet Union. The Communists had a lot of support from the working classes and close links with the Soviet Union. Many people in Germany began to fear the Communists would take over the country. In particular, German business owners and farmers feared the Communists because in the Soviet Union the Communist government had taken over big industries and farmers' land.

## B

## WEAK OPPOSITION

**Weak opposition.** The Nazis were also fortunate that their opponents were so weak. Stronger opposition would have made it a lot more difficult for the Nazis to get into power.

Opposition to the Nazis was weak and divided. The Nazis' two main rivals, the Communist Party and the Social Democratic Party, were bitter enemies. They were not prepared to work together to stop the Nazis.

People had lost trust in the parties that had ruled Germany during the Great Depression. These parties did not seem to be able to do anything to solve the crisis. To make matters worse, they argued amongst themselves about what to do. They did not offer strong, effective leadership.

Finally, we must remember that Hitler became Chancellor because of a **political deal** with the leader of another party. Without this deal he woud not have been able to become Chancellor. Whether or not Hitler became Chancellor remained in the balance until the very last moment.

**C**

## A POLITICAL DEAL

**1 NAZI SUCCESS**
In July 1932 the Nazis won 37 per cent of the vote in the elections. They were the largest party in the Reichstag. However, the Nazis did not have the majority they needed to control the Reichstag.

**2 ENTER PAPEN**
Hitler demanded to be made Chancellor. However, Paul von Hindenburg (the President) refused. Instead, he appointed his friend, Franz von Papen (leader of the Centre Party), as Chancellor. Papen soon faced many problems. He did not have the support of the Reichstag.

**3 ENTER SCHLEICHER**
General von Schleicher persuaded Hindenburg to remove Papen. In December, Schleicher became Chancellor, but he failed to gain the support of the Reichstag.

**4 PAPEN'S REVENGE!**
Papen wanted revenge. The Nazis were still the largest party so Papen thought he could use them to get power for himself and remove Schleicher. He made a deal with Hitler. They agreed to form a new government, with Hitler as Chancellor and Papen as Vice-Chancellor. Wealthy businessmen went along with the plan because they believed that Papen, not Hitler, would control the new government.

**5 ENTER HITLER**
Papen persuaded Hindenburg to agree to his plan. In January 1933 Hitler became Chancellor. Hindenburg and Papen thought they could control Hitler. They made sure only three out of the twelve people who made up the new government were Nazis.

# Why did some Germans change their minds and vote for Hitler?

Why might people who would not have supported the Nazis in 1928 have changed their minds by 1932?

**Discuss**

Here are the five people whom you first met on page 33. Study what has happened to each of them between 1928 and 1932.
a) Which people who would not have supported the Nazis in 1928 might support them now? Why do you think their views might have changed?
b) Which people who would not have supported the Nazis in 1928 would still not do so now? Why do you think their views would not have changed?

**Dietrich**

I have lost my job working in the factory. Like most of my friends I am now unemployed. My landlord has kicked me out of my flat because I could not afford the rent. The government is doing nothing to help. They don't care about people like me. The Nazis are the only party who seem to be doing anything. The SA have been running soup kitchens and they have put some of my friends up in a hostel.

**Josef**

My business is really struggling. People just don't have the money to spend any more. Demand for goods has dropped and so have my profits. I have had to lay off a lot of workers. The situation at the moment really scares me. Hitler blames the crisis on the Jews. With so much bitterness and anger about, people are starting to listen to him. They want someone to blame. I am worried about the safety of my family.

**Maria**

I have not been able to get a job since I left university. I am well-qualified, but with so much unemployment there is little hope for people like me. My boyfriend and I are living in a tent in the local park whilst the rich still live life to the full. The only good news is that support for the Communists is growing. The Nazis keep trying to break up our meetings but many workers are starting to listen to our message.

**Franz**

**Helga**

My husband's factory has gone bankrupt. The loans that he depended on stopped after the Wall Street Crash. Many of the banks have gone bankrupt too. There is no hope of my husband raising enough money to set up another business. We're having to live off our savings. The government is useless. The different parties spend too long arguing amongst themselves. What we need is a strong leader who can sort out the mess that we are in. Gangs of workers hang around on the streets and there is a lot of violence. I really fear that the Communists could take over. People are desperate and are starting to look for drastic alternatives.

The farmer that I used to work for has gone bankrupt. Food prices had been falling for a number of years. The depression made the situation even worse. It was impossible for small farms such as his to survive. I am grateful that he kept me on as long as he did. I have moved in with my parents because I cannot afford a house of my own. It is hard for my parents. They help me out as much as they can, but the government has cut their pension payments again.

# Meet the Examiner: Spotting icebergs

Look at this iceberg question:

> How important was the Wall Street Crash, amongst other factors, in bringing Hitler to power in 1933? [12]

You need to be careful with this type of question. It usually appears as the final question on your exam paper, at the end of Section B. Like an iceberg there is more to it than meets the eye! Many students think that a question such as this requires them to write *only* about the Wall Street Crash. This would be very dangerous.

Look at the question closely. You have to explore *'how important'* the Wall Street Crash was as a factor in Hitler's rise to power. To do this properly you must **examine the role played by other factors as well**.

To gain the highest level mark you also need to **weigh the relative importance of the Wall Street Crash against these other factors**. Was it the most important factor or were other factors more important?

Follow the steps below to safely negotiate this iceberg question!

BEWARE OF ICEBERG QUESTIONS

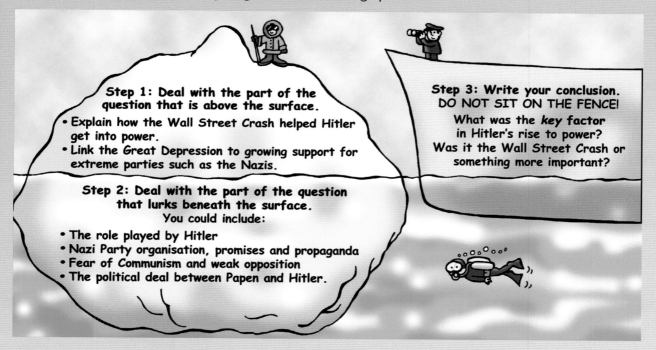

**Step 1: Deal with the part of the question that is above the surface.**
- Explain how the Wall Street Crash helped Hitler get into power.
- Link the Great Depression to growing support for extreme parties such as the Nazis.

**Step 2: Deal with the part of the question that lurks beneath the surface.**
You could include:
- The role played by Hitler
- Nazi Party organisation, promises and propaganda
- Fear of Communism and weak opposition
- The political deal between Papen and Hitler.

**Step 3: Write your conclusion. DO NOT SIT ON THE FENCE!**
What was the *key factor* in Hitler's rise to power? Was it the Wall Street Crash or something more important?

## Extra advice

**Add a 'turning the corner' connective**
Aim for three paragraphs. When you begin your second paragraph (see step two above) you should start with a strong 'turning-the-corner' connective to show that you have not hit the iceberg and that you can see that there is more to the question than meets the eye. Here is an example:

> *However, the Wall Street Crash was not the only factor that helped Hitler get into power. The Nazi party was very well organised and used propaganda very effectively. For example ...'*

## 2.1 How was Hitler able to become dictator?

In January 1933 Hitler became Chancellor of Germany. By August 1934 democracy in Germany was dead and Hitler was dictator. How did he do this? You will discover the sequence of events that brought this about and make a 'living graph' of Nazi power to show how Hitler was able to destroy democracy.

### How strong was Hitler's position in January 1933?

When Hitler became Chancellor he was in a very weak position.

- Support for the Nazis had fallen from 37 per cent to 33 per cent during 1932. In order to control the Reichstag, Hitler needed over 50 per cent of the vote. He was a long way from achieving this.
- Hitler could be sacked by President Hindenburg at any time.
- Apart from Hitler, only two other Nazis had been given positions in the new government. The nine other positions were filled by non-Nazis whom Hindenburg and Papen thought they could control.
- Hindenburg and Papen planned to use Hitler like a puppet. Papen boasted to a friend, 'In two months we will have pushed Hitler into a corner so that he squeaks'.

### 18 months later …

By the end of 1934 Hitler was in a totally different position.

- Papen had resigned.
- Hindenburg was dead and Hitler was now President, as well as Chancellor.
- The army had taken an oath of personal loyalty to Hitler.
- The Nazis were the only political party.
- All threats to the Nazi Party had been removed.
- Hitler had the power to introduce any law he wanted.

How did this happen?

THE REICHSTAG
THE ARMY
THE MEDIA
THE GERMAN PEOPLE
THE LAW
TRADE UNIONS
LOCAL GOVERNMENT

To be successful in your GCSE exam to you need to create overviews of key periods within the Enquiry in Depth. As you have seen on page 44, the period from January 1933 to August 1934 was a crucial period in which Hitler moved from being a weak Chancellor to an all-powerful dictator. Producing a living graph is a very good way of studying this important part of the course.

## Activity

Using information from pages 46–47, you are going to construct a living graph like this, which charts how Hitler increased his power between January 1933 and August 1934.

- You will need to use A3 paper.
- Think carefully about where you plot each event.
- Use bullet points to explain your thinking and support the decisions you make.

When you have finished, answer the following questions.

1 Which of the following periods do you think was the most important:

- February 1933–March 1933
- May 1933–July 1933
- June 1934–August 1934?

Write a sentence to explain your answer.

2 Mark on your living graph three turning points that led to a significant increase in Hitler's power. Rank them in order of importance and write a paragraph to explain your decision.

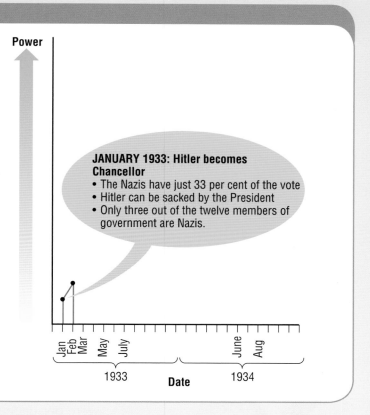

**JANUARY 1933: Hitler becomes Chancellor**
- The Nazis have just 33 per cent of the vote
- Hitler can be sacked by the President
- Only three out of the twelve members of government are Nazis.

You can use living graphs to revise other parts of the course. For example, you could use different colours to plot the popularity of the Weimar Republic and the Nazi Party from 1920 to 1933.

# Hitler's path to dictatorship

1933

## 27 February – Reichstag fire

The Reichstag building in Berlin was destroyed by fire. Marinus van der Lubbe, a Dutch Communist, was found at the scene. He appeared to have been acting alone but the Nazis claimed that this was the start of a Communist plot to take over Germany. That night 4000 Communist leaders were arrested by the police. The next day Hitler persuaded Hindenburg to grant him emergency powers. This gave the police the power to arrest people and hold them for as long as they wanted, without trial. Thousands of people who opposed the Nazi Party were arrested. The Nazis also banned meetings held by their political opponents and closed down their newspapers.

## 5 March – New elections

The Nazis used the police and the SA to put pressure on their political opponents. More than 50 opponents of the Nazis were killed and many more were injured. The Nazis used radio to broadcast their anti-Communist message. This helped the Nazis achieve their best ever election result, with 44 per cent of the vote.

## 24 March – The Enabling Law

Hitler wanted still more. He wanted an Enabling Law. This law would give Hitler the power to pass laws without going through the Reichstag or the President. It would place all the power in his hands. In order to achieve this he needed to get two-thirds of the Reichstag to support it. They had to be persuaded to give up their power and hand it to Hitler! How did he achieve this?

The Communist Party were banned from voting. The Centre Party were persuaded to vote in favour of the law as Hitler promised to protect the Catholic Church. Only the Social Democrats voted against it. The Enabling Law was passed by 444 votes to 94.

The Weimar Republic and the democracy it brought to Germany had ended. The Reichstag had voted itself out of existence. Germany was now a dictatorship. All important decisions would be made by Hitler and his closest advisers.

## 2 May – Trade unions taken over

Trade union offices were taken over and union leaders arrested. All trade unions were merged into one organisation, the new German Labour Front (DAF). The DAF was controlled by the Nazis.

## July – All political parties banned

A law was introduced that banned people from forming new political parties. By this stage the Social Democratic Party and the Communist Party had already been banned. Other political parties had broken up. This new law meant that no new parties could be set up to challenge the Nazis. There was now only one party in Germany.

**Communist Party Manifesto BANNED**

**German Democratic Party Manifesto BANNED**

**Social Democratic Party Manifesto BANNED**

1934

## 29–30 June – Night of the Long Knives

By 1934 Hitler had become concerned at the increasing power of the SA. It had over 3 million members and wanted to take control of the army. The leader of the SA, Ernst Röhm, was a close friend of Hitler's. However, Hitler thought that Röhm was a potential rival.

Hitler had another reason for attacking the SA. He needed to reassure the army. The army was smaller than the SA but it was well-trained and disciplined. It was the only organisation that had the power to overthrow Hitler. Army leaders feared being taken over by the SA and resented the violence they used. The army was supported by powerful businessmen who wanted Hitler to expand the army and buy new weapons.

On the Night of the Long Knives, SA leaders were dragged from their beds, taken to Nazi headquarters and shot dead. Röhm too was arrested. When he refused to commit suicide, he was shot in prison. The Night of the Long Knives sent a warning to the rest of Germany about how ruthless Hitler was in his pursuit of power.

## 2 August – Death of Hindenburg

When Hindenburg died, Hitler made himself President as well as Chancellor. He was now the undisputed head of the government and took the title *Führer* (Supreme Leader).

## August – Army oath

The army took an oath of personal loyalty to Hitler. Hitler was now Supreme Commander of the armed forces. All German soldiers swore to obey Hitler and to risk their life for him at any time.

How were Hitler and the Nazi Party able to increase their power between January 1933 and August 1934? [10]

This is a very important question. In the space of just eighteen months Hitler was able to go from being a weak Chancellor to being an all-powerful dictator. You have to **explain how** this dramatic change took place. It is also a difficult question. That is why it is worth 10 marks.

First of all, a warning! The danger with this question is that you could end up telling a story. Look at how the student here has started to answer the question. Each paragraph describes what happened but does not **explain how** this helped Hitler increase his power.

## Avoid danger … use connectives!

In answering the question, the aim is to link events with their results. You can do this by using **result connectives** in each paragraph. You can see some examples of this below. Result connectives can help you tie your answer together. They make sure that you **explain why** something took place rather than just telling a story.

### Useful result connectives

This meant that …
This led to …
It enabled him to …
He could now …
This resulted in …

In January 1933 Hitler was in a weak position. President Hindenburg could sack him at any time and he had only 33 per cent of the vote. In February 1933 the Reichstag was burnt down by a Dutch Communist called Marinus van der Lubbe. The Nazis claimed that this was part of a Communist plot to take over Germany.

This meant that Hitler was able to persuade Hindenburg to grant him Emergency Powers. Hitler used these powers to attack Communists and political opponents. This led to the Nazis achieving their best ever election result in March 1933.

In the March 1933 election the Nazis gained 44 per cent of the vote but Hitler still did not have the majority he wanted in the Reichstag. However, later in the month he persuaded the Reichstag to pass the Enabling Law.

This meant that … (Explain the Enabling Law and why it was so important.)

In May Hitler took over the trade unions and in July he banned all other political parties.

The new powers of the Enabling Law resulted in Hitler being able to …

## Activity

Answer the exam question.
- You can use the student's attempt as a starting point.
- Make sure you improve what the student has written for the first three paragraphs by using the result connectives to help you explain the importance of each development. Some result connectives are given on page 48.
- Three paragraphs is enough, but if you want to write more you could look at:
  - the Night of the Long Knives
  - Hindenburg's death
  - the army's oath of loyalty.
- Finally, write a conclusion, but read the advice below first.

## What makes a good conclusion to an 'explanation' question?

The conclusion is a very important part of your answer. In the exam question you answered on page 43, you were encouraged to give your opinion. Questions that ask you to explain how or why something happened are just the same. The examiner is interested in your opinion. Use the conclusion to put forward a clear line of argument. Explain which events or developments you think were the most important causes. Don't sit on the fence!

Many students make the mistake of thinking that a good conclusion is a summary of what they have written in the main part of their essay. They often repeat what they have already said! Try to avoid this. Aim to write less but think more! A good conclusion can be as little as two or three sentences.

For this exam question try to identify one or two key turning points which really helped Hitler to increase his power. You might want to use one of these sentence starters to begin your conclusion:

*The key event that helped Hitler to increase his power was ...*
*Without ... Hitler would not have been able to ...*

## 2.2 How effectively did the Nazis control Germany between 1933 and 1945?

**Discuss**

Which part of Himmler's terror network do you think was most important?

Hitler did not rule Germany on his own. In fact, he didn't work very hard. He made important decisions but other people carried them out. These were 'Hitler's henchmen': the powerful people who actually ran the Nazi empire. These Nazis tried to make the German people feel too afraid to express any kind of criticism or opposition. At the centre of this network of fear was Heinrich Himmler, one of Hitler's most important henchmen. How effectively did Himmler and his terror network control Germany? Did anyone dare oppose Nazi rule?

### The SS

SS stands for 'Schutz Staffel', which means protection squad. The black-uniformed SS was originally Hitler's personal bodyguard. Himmler built it up and by 1939 it had 240,000 members. All recruits had to be recognisably 'Aryan' – blonde, blue-eyed and physically fit. Himmler imposed high physical standards: even having a filled tooth was enough to disqualify you. Himmler trained the SS to be ruthless and fiercely loyal to Hitler. They could arrest people without trial and could search houses.

### Concentration camps

As soon as the Nazi Party came to power the SS arrested many Nazi opponents and put them in temporary prisons. Then special concentration camps were constructed, usually in remote rural areas.

At first, inmates were held in the camps for short periods of questioning, torture, hard labour and forced instruction in Nazi ideas. By the late 1930s concentration camps were being run by a section of the SS called Death's Head units, as forced labour camps. Some prisoners were used to work for Nazi-owned businesses. Himmler controlled over 150 companies who used slave labour to make all kinds of goods, including weapons.

The camps held Jews, Communists, Socialists, trade unionists, church leaders – anyone who criticised the Nazis.

**Source 1**

▲ Nazi opponents being questioned in a concentration camp, 1933

## The Gestapo

This was the state secret police. They could tap telephones, open mail and collect information from a huge network of informers. Informers reported on local people who they believed were 'anti-Nazi'. The Gestapo arrested people without trial, tortured them and imprisoned them in concentration camps.

## The police and the courts

The ordinary **police** continued with their regular work, but their bosses were all Nazis. This meant that the police became part of the network of informers, collecting information on everyone, whilst ignoring crimes committed by Nazis.

The **courts** were under Nazi control as well. Nazis were appointed as judges so a fair trial was impossible. The number of offences carrying the death penalty went up from three in 1933 to 46 by 1943. These included: listening to foreign radio stations; telling an anti-Nazi joke; having a sexual relationship with a Jew; and being a habitual criminal.

### Source 2

▲ A teletype room in Gestapo headquarters, where information was received from informers

### Source 3

▲ German judges give the Nazi salute as they swear loyalty to Hitler

## Informers

The Nazi Party had a strong local structure. Every town was divided into small units, called blocks. The Block Warden, a local Nazi, visited every home in the block each week, collecting donations to the Nazi Party and checking up on everyone.

As a Socialist opponent of Hitler said, 'Every staircase has an informer.' The Block Warden wrote a report on everyone in their block. This report could affect whether or not you got a job. The Warden noted any signs of independent thinking, for example, not flying the Nazi flag on celebration days, or not being enthusiastic enough about Hitler and his achievements.

# How big a threat did opposition groups pose to the Nazis?

You may have the impression that there was no opposition to the Nazis at all, but that was not the case. On pages 53–56 you will find out about four different opposition groups. You will think about why each one was opposed to Hitler and which one posed the biggest threat to Nazi power.

The Nazis did not want any opposition. In their ideal Germany all Germans would work together to achieve the same goals – the Nazi goals. Within days of taking power Hitler banned all other political parties. The normal democratic right to oppose or protest against a government was not going to be allowed.

## The Gestapo

As we saw on page 51, the Gestapo made it their business to find out about Nazi opponents. They tapped phones, opened letters and spied on suspects. A network of Nazi informers passed on information to them. Suspected opponents were arrested and, if part of a wider network, were tortured until they revealed the names of everyone in their group.

### Activity

On the next four pages you will find Gestapo 'information files' about each opposition group. As you read them, think about how much of a threat each one posed to Hitler and the Nazis. Complete your own copy of this table and give each group a 'danger rating' (!!!!! = very dangerous; ! = no threat at all).

## GESTAPO SECRET FILE

| Group | Methods used to oppose the Nazis | Danger rating | Reasons why you have given that score |
|---|---|---|---|
| Former political opponents | | | |
| The Churches | | | |
| Army officers | | | |
| White Rose Group | | | |

## GESTAPO SECRET FILE

### OPPOSITION GROUPS
### 1 Former political opponents

**SUPPORT:** The Socialist Party, the Communist Party and the trade unions. They were, of course, our main enemies in the Weimar Republic. They were huge organisations in those days. The parties lost the elections of 1933 but still have millions of members. So do the trade unions.

**AIMS:** Restoration of democracy, free speech and workers' democratic rights. The Communists want a workers' revolution.

**ACTIVITIES:** Secret meetings, strikes, handing out leaflets, writing anti-Nazi graffiti on walls.

**WHEN MOST ACTIVE:** 1933–1935

## What happened …

All opposition parties and trade unions were banned by July 1933. Their offices were raided, ransacked and closed. Thousands of Socialists, including members of the Reichstag and former ministers as well as trade union officials, were arrested and put in concentration camps. Many were beaten up; some were tortured; a few were killed. Most were soon released. The aim was to scare people into joining the Nazis, or at least into keeping quiet.

In the years immediately after 1933, working-class opposition to Nazism continued: from 1933 to 1935 there were 400 strikes. However, the Gestapo continued to make mass arrests – for example, two-thirds of all Communist Party members were arrested. Many died in the camps. Many more went into exile abroad. Socialist, Communist and trade union organisations were forced underground, holding secret meetings, occasionally handing out leaflets, waiting for the day when democracy would return to Germany.

Source 4

◄ Political prisoners in a concentration camp near Berlin

## GESTAPO SECRET FILE

### OPPOSITION GROUPS
### 2 The Churches

**SUPPORT:** About 22 million people belong to the Roman Catholic Church – 32 per cent of the population. About 40 million belong to Protestant Churches – 58 per cent of the population. There are other, smaller Christian Churches, too.

The Churches are by far the largest non-Nazi organisation left in Germany after 1933. They have bishops to lead them and a priest or pastor in every parish, to whom many ordinary Germans look for guidance.

**AIMS:** These are large organisations embracing a variety of political views. Some Church leaders actively support the Nazis, some actively oppose them. Most are somewhere in-between and want to keep religion and politics separate. Some just want to keep their important positions.

**ACTIVITIES:** They carry out baptisms, marriages and burials. The Churches also run many schools: two-thirds of all German children go to a Church school.

**WHEN MOST ACTIVE:** Throughout the whole Nazi period, 1933–1945.

## What happened …

Only when Hitler interfered with the activities of the Churches, for example by shutting down youth groups, did many religious leaders object.

Overall, Church opposition to the Nazis did not go very far: they did not, for example, criticise the attacks on Jewish people and property that took place on Kristallnacht. Only 50 pastors (out of 17,000) and one bishop were actually put in prison for opposition activities or speeches.

**Martin Niemöller** was a First World War hero as a U-boat captain. During the 1930s he became an open critic of the Nazis. Niemöller was one of the founders of the Confessional Church. The Nazis had set up a 'Reich Church' in which pastors had to swear an oath of loyalty to Hitler. Many refused and by 1934 6000 Protestant pastors had left the Reich Church and joined the new, non-Nazi, Confessional Church that Niemöller had helped to establish. Niemöller was arrested in 1937 and spent the rest of the Nazi years in a concentration camp.

**Dietrich Bonhöffer** pointed out that Nazism was anti-Christian as early as 1933. His job was training young men to be ministers. He taught them that one cannot, and should not, separate religion and politics and that true religion is standing up to a corrupt or evil government. The Nazis closed his college in 1940. He could have escaped to Britain, where he had many friends, but chose to stay and speak out against Nazism. He was arrested in 1943 and executed in 1945. His ideas have been influential throughout the world since his death.

# GESTAPO SECRET FILE

## OPPOSITION GROUPS
### 3 Army officers

**SUPPORT:** A group of army officers.
**AIMS:** To replace Hitler and seize power.
**ACTIVITIES:** Attempting to assassinate Hitler.
**WHEN MOST ACTIVE:** 1943–1944.

## What happened …

Many upper-class Germans were scornful of Hitler, with his lower-class origins and street-fighting past. They had supported the Kaiser and traditionally served in the army, as officers. Hitler bought the support of the army in 1934 by weakening the SA in the Night of the Long Knives (page 47). However, Hitler's racial policies horrified many of the officer class. Many of them were against Hitler's rush to war in 1939 and opposed the invasion of the USSR in 1941 (page 69). They were horrified by the brutal actions of the SS in eastern Europe, which were against their strict code of honour in war. They also resented Hitler meddling in military strategy. When victory turned to defeat in 1943 (page 69), they decided that Hitler had to be removed.

There were said to be dozens of plots to assassinate Hitler. The one that came nearest to success was organised by Claus von Stauffenberg, who planted a bomb in Hitler's military headquarters in July 1944.

Claus von Stauffenberg had been a Nazi supporter in the 1930s because he thought that Hitler was the best person to stop the Communists. However, he was disgusted by the Nazis' anti-Semitism and by 1943 thought that Hitler was leading Germany to a catastrophic defeat in the Second World War. He therefore decided to plant a bomb at a meeting he knew Hitler would be attending. Army officers would then seize power in Berlin. All his carefully made plans went well, except for some tiny – and crucial – details:

- the meeting was not held in an underground bunker, but in a large single-story building. It was a hot day and the windows were left open. This meant that the force of the blast was lessened

**Source 5**

▲ Hitler's bombed conference room, July 1944

- after Stauffenberg left the room, someone moved the briefcase containing the bomb slightly further away from Hitler.

The bomb went off. Four people were killed – but not Hitler, who was only injured. Stauffenberg rushed to Berlin, but the other plotters had not acted. All the plotters were rounded up and executed. Hitler used the failed plot as an excuse to round up all of his known opponents, whether they were part of the bomb plot or not. As a result 5000 people were arrested and executed.

## GESTAPO SECRET FILE

### OPPOSITION GROUPS
### 4 Young people: the White Rose Group

**SUPPORT:** A small group of students at Munich University led by Hans Scholl, Sophie Scholl and Christoph Probst.

**AIMS:** To shame the German people by protesting against the Nazis. To urge Germans to sabotage the war effort and overthrow Hitler.

**ACTIVITIES:** Spreading anti-Nazi messages through handing out leaflets, putting up posters and writing graffiti on walls.

**WHEN MOST ACTIVE:** Summer 1942; Jan–Feb 1943.

### Source 6

▲ The White Rose Group (left to right: Hans Scholl, Sophie Scholl, Christoph Probst)

## What happened ...

The White Rose Group were disgusted at the lack of opposition to the Nazis and their persecution of the Jews. Sophie Scholl wrote: 'Germany's name will be disgraced forever unless German youth finally rises up, takes revenge, smashes its torturers and builds a new, spiritual Europe'. Hans and Sophie were arrested and tortured before being executed (see below).

### Source A

Article in a German newspaper, 22 February 1943:

On 22 February 1943, the People's Court sentenced to death the following persons:
Hans Scholl, aged 24; Sophie Scholl, aged 21. The sentence was carried out the same day. Typical outsiders, these two people shamelessly committed offences against the security of Germany, by painting slogans on houses and distributing leaflets. At this time of heroic struggle on the part of the German people, these despicable criminals deserve a speedy and dishonourable death.

### Source B

Extract from a radio programme broadcast on 27 June 1943 by the famous German writer, Thomas Mann, whilst in exile in Britain. Thomas Mann left Germany in 1933:

Hans and Sophie Scholl put their heads on the block for the love of Germany. They went to their death after telling the judge at court to his face that 'soon you will be standing here where we now stand'. Good splendid young people! You shall not have died in vain; you shall not be forgotten. The Nazis have built monuments to common killers in Germany – but the German revolution will tear them down and replace them with people like you.

### Source C

Extract from a leaflet issued by the National Committee for a Free Germany:

A short time ago we heard the terrible news that two young Germans, Hans and his sister Sophie Scholl, were executed at the end of February. They belonged to a group of noble and courageous young Germans who refused to put up with the terrible sufferings of Nazi Germany any longer. They were the first to raise the flag of freedom.
The axe of the Hitler executioner was raised two times; two times it fell; and two young heads rolled from the block. Two heroes died, but their struggle for German freedom lives on in the hearts of millions of young Germans.

Your GCSE History exam is divided into two sections. Section A is worth 36 marks and Section B is worth 24 marks. This page focuses on the type of questions that appear in Section A.

- You should aim to spend approximately one hour on Section A which is made up of five questions.
- Question 1 is usually an **inference** question. We have already looked at how to approach this type of question (see pages 26–27). You can practise your skills with the sample question below.
- Questions 2 and 3 test your ability to compare sources. You can use the advice below to help you tackle the two sample questions.
- Question 4 asks you to evaluate how useful a source is for a particular enquiry. We will look at this question type on pages 88–89.
- Question 5 is an essay-style question. It will be similar in style to the question we looked at on pages 48–49.

## Source D

▲ The public hanging of twelve Edelweiss Pirates who opposed the Nazis in Cologne in 1944 (see page 72)

### Section A

**1 (a)** What do **Sources A** and **D** suggest about Nazi attitudes to opposition groups? [4]

**(b)** What different view of opposition groups is suggested by **Sources B** and **C**? [6]

**(c)** Why do you think **Source A** gives a different view of the White Rose Group to **Sources B** and **C**? Explain your answer using Sources A, B and C and your own knowledge. [8]

## Cross-referencing sources

Question 1b is asking you to compare what is being said in two sources. This skill is known as cross-referencing.

**Step 1: Annotate the source**. Use your inference skills to identify the key messages in each source. Remember to highlight the key details in each source first (see pages 26–27).

**Step 2**: When you write your answer **make direct comparisons**. You will not get high marks if you simply describe what Source A says, then describe what Source B says. Instead you should aim to make direct comparisons as you go through your answer. For example:

*'Source A argues that Hans and Sophie Scholl are ...*
*In contrast Source B ...'*

## Explaining why sources give different views

Question 1c is different from 1b. Here you need to explain why the two sources contain different views of the White Rose Group. Look carefully at the provenance of the source. Consider the **Five Ws**:

- **What** type of source is it?
- **When** was it produced?
- **Who** produced the source?
- **Why** was it written? What are the likely motives of the person writing the source?
- **Where** was it written?

# Why didn't many Germans oppose the Nazis?

Look back over the four groups of opponents and the danger rating you gave them for the Activity on page 52. Compare your scores with others in the class. Did you give anyone the highest rating? Probably not!

One of the hardest things to explain when you study Nazi Germany is why there was not more opposition. This is what you are going to work on now. Start with these four ordinary Germans and their answers to the question: 'Why don't I oppose the Nazis?'

## Activity

You are going to create your own diagram to sum up the reasons why opposition to the Nazis was so weak.

1   Write Wilhelm's name in the middle of a piece of paper. Write the words 'Terror', 'Isolation', 'Nazi achievements' and 'Propaganda' around his name.

2   Read what Wilhelm says. How important do you think each of these four factors was in explaining Wilhelm's failure to oppose the Nazis? Draw lines between Wilhelm and the factors. Use a thick, bold line for the most important factor, and a thin, faint line for less important factors.

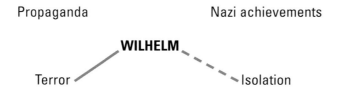

Propaganda                    Nazi achievements

**WILHELM**

Terror                          Isolation

3   Look for links between the factors. Draw links between factors, using thick and bold or thin and faint lines depending on how strong you think the links were.

4   Now draw three more charts for Hermann, Maria and Kitty.

> I don't like the Nazis, but I'm scared to say so to anyone else. I know exactly what happens to those who do: the Gestapo calls on them one night and they disappear.
>
> They get beaten to death in the police station, or on the way there, or in a concentration camp. I daren't say what I think. The local Nazi boss – a dreadful fat lout, used to be a butcher's assistant, no manners at all – knows I don't like them. He's looking for a chance to get me. He even offered one of my servants a thousand marks for any information which could lead to my arrest. My beautiful Germany has been over-run by these pigs! But I've got my estate to manage and my family and servants to think of. I really dare not speak out.

**Wilhelm**

> Sometimes I get worried about what the Nazis are doing, but then when I hear them explain things it all makes sense again.
>
> My older brother is in the Hitler Youth and gets to go to big torchlight rallies: he says it's a wonderful experience, swept along by the huge crowd all working for the same thing. It's on the radio too: my mum and I listen to Goebbels telling us all the great things Hitler and the Nazis have done and how they're going to make Germany even better. Of course, some bad people have been locked up, but Hitler says they deserved it – and I trust Hitler. My dad reads the papers and he says, 'Why should we want to change things when the Nazis are getting everything right? We had all that argument under Weimar and look where it got us.'

**Hermann**

I like the Nazis. I think Hitler is the best thing that has happened to Germany for years.

Look what the Nazis have achieved. Look how they have built up our army and navy again. Other countries won't be putting us down so much now! And unemployment – those layabouts are being made to work instead of living off the dole. There's order on the streets now – none of the noise and violence we had to put up with under that awful Weimar government. The Nazis are organised and focused and Hitler is the strong man we need. Of course, to set Germany straight again has meant taking a firm line with some people, like those Communists who want a revolution here, as in the USSR. They deserve to be locked up. So do all the other bad elements Hitler has removed.

# WHY DON'T I OPPOSE THE NAZIS?

**Maria**

I hate the Nazis but what can I do? Since the other political parties have been banned there is nowhere to turn. I feel like I am on my own.

I used to read the Socialist newspaper, but it stopped soon after the Nazis took over. The Socialist rallies and meetings I used to go to don't happen any more. Most of the great speakers, organisers and leaders we used to rely on have gone. Many have died in those awful Nazi camps. There are some old friends I can talk to, of course. We have a grumble and crack a few jokes. But I'm not a heroine: I can't go underground, or sabotage the war factories, much as I'd like to. I wouldn't know how, and I've got my old mother and three children to look after. But we're not going to get rid of Hitler by cracking anti-Nazi jokes. There's no one to lead us any more. We feel so weak, useless and disorganised.

**Kitty**

# 3.1 How much change did the Nazis bring about in German society?

Hitler had very clear ideas about how everyone fitted into his Nazi future. Young people, women and workers had important roles but Jews and others soon discovered that they had no place in Nazi society. You will find out about some of these people and decide how much the Nazis really changed people's lives.

## Hitler's Germany

Hitler had very clear ideas about the kind of Germany he wanted.

**A Germany with the Nazi Party in control**
It was not the job of the German people to vote, or criticise; they had simply to obey and be grateful.

**A racially pure Germany**
Only Aryans – the blond-haired, blue-eyed and pale-skinned – would be welcome.

**A Germany with traditional roles for men and women**
Women, wearing simple clothes and no make-up, would stay at home, cook simple meals and produce babies.
Men would work and, if necessary, fight.
Boys and girls would be prepared for their different roles through the education system.

Source 1

▲ A Nazi propaganda poster from the 1930s. At the top it says: 'The NSDAP (Nazi Party) protects the national community.' At the bottom it says: 'People: if you need help, go to your local Party group'

### Discuss

1 What does Source 1 tell you about each of the three big Nazi ideas:
   a) racial purity
   b) traditional roles for men and women
   c) the role of the Nazi Party?
2 What else does it suggest to you about Nazi rule?

### Activity

Look at the four Germans on the opposite page. Draw a table to show how the Nazi ideas might change each person's life. Create a row each for Hans, Karl, Gudrun and Lisa, and add three columns, headed **Their lives in 1933**, **Your prediction: changes likely in their lives under Nazi rule**, and **What really happened**.
1 In the first column, write three points about the life of each person in 1933.
2 How do you think their lives might change under Nazi rule? Put these ideas in column 2.
3 Which person do you think is going to be affected most by Nazi rule?
You should leave column 3 blank for now. Fill that in later as you work through Sections 3 and 4.

# Life in Germany, 1933

Here are four Germans, talking about themselves in 1933. Hitler has just become ruler of Germany.

**Karl**

I'm Karl and I live in Dortmund. I'm a metal worker. I've got twenty years' experience at a lathe, so I know what I'm doing. Or I would, if I had a job. Like millions of others I'm out of work now and I hate seeing my family scraping by on unemployment benefits. I didn't vote for Hitler. I can't see that he's going to be able to pull Germany out of this mess.

My name is Hans and I'm thirteen years old. I live in a small town with my parents and my younger sister, Anna. I like playing with my friends, although I wish there was more for us to do here. I'm trying to do well at school; times are hard and my father has just lost his job so I want to be able to get work when I grow up. I'm hearing the grown-ups talk a lot about Hitler these days, but I don't suppose he'll make much difference to my life.

**Hans**

**Gudrun**

My name is Gudrun and I live in Berlin. I'm a senior hospital doctor. After the war, when the Weimar Republic replaced the old Kaiser's rule, the situation for women improved a lot. We got the vote, equal pay and equal rights at work. There were much better opportunities for women to make a career. I'm married, but my husband and I decided to have just one child so that I could get back to work. I've heard Hitler ranting his old-fashioned views on women but I can't think he's really going to put the clock back.

**Lisa**

My name is Lisa and I'm starting university next year. I'm Jewish. My family have lived here, in Frankfurt, for centuries. My father fought for our country in the War and was gassed, so he can't work much. I'm a bit scared by some of the things Hitler says about the Jews and I could hardly believe it when a man like that became Chancellor. But my Granny says, 'The soup's usually not served as hot as it's cooked.' I hope she's right.

# How did the Nazis change the lives of women?

**Gudrun**

1939

The Nazis were very old-fashioned in their attitude to women. They wanted women to be mothers not workers. These are some of the methods they used to try to achieve this:

'I have given a child to the Führer!' These are the words I heard a German woman call out after giving birth. This was just what Hitler wanted from women like me.

## Out!

All women employed by the state – doctors, civil servants and many teachers – were sacked. In appointing new staff, men were preferred to women.

## Loans

Loans were offered to couples to encourage them to get married. They received 1000 marks, or about a half year's pay. The more children they had, the less they had to pay back. If they had four children they paid nothing back. But there was one condition: the woman had to leave her job.

## Medals

Medals were awarded for having children: gold for eight; silver for six; bronze for four (see Source 3).

However, not everyone was allowed to have children. It was compulsory for women with inherited diseases, or weaknesses such as colour-blindness, to be sterilised.

## Propaganda

In line with their old-fashioned ideas the Nazis also wanted women to wear simple, rather than fashionable, clothes. Wearing trousers or high heels, having permed or dyed hair, using make-up or smoking in public were all frowned upon. Some Nazis got restaurants to ban women from smoking and 'good Nazis' were encouraged to tell off any fashionably-dressed women in public.

Slimming was also frowned upon as the Nazis wanted women to be strong and solid in order to have lots of babies.

Since it is not easy to pass laws about many of these things, the Nazis tried to persuade women to follow their ideals by using massive amounts of propaganda, such as leaflets (Source 4) and posters (Sources 1 [page 60] and 5). Women were urged to follow the 'Three Ks': Kinder, Kirche, Küche (children, church, cooking).

### Source 3

▲ The 'Honour Cross of the German Mother'

## Source 4

From a Nazi leaflet issued to young German women:

1 Remember that you are a German!
2 If you are healthy, do not stay single!
3 Keep your body pure!
4 Keep your mind and spirit pure!
5 Marry only for love!
6 As a German, choose only a husband of the same blood!
7 In choosing a husband, ask about his forebears [ancestors]!
8 Health is essential to beauty!
9 Don't look for a playmate but for a companion!
10 You should want to have as many children as possible!

## Activity

1 The Nazi campaign to force women to follow their ideals was based on 'sticks and carrots'; that is, sticks to punish them if they did undesirable things and carrots to encourage them to do what the Nazis wanted. Which of the measures described on page 62 are 'sticks' and which are 'carrots'?

2 Choose the opposite point of view to the Nazis on one of these topics. Design a poster to persuade women to agree with you.

3 Look back to Gudrun in 1933 on page 61. How do you think Nazi rule would have affected her life? In column 3 of your table list the changes that took place.

4 Mark each change out of 5 for how serious you think it is (5 = very serious, 1 = trivial).

5 Are any of the changes for the better for Gudrun?

## Source 5

▲ A Nazi poster from 1935. It says: 'Germany grows through strong mothers and healthy children'

## HOWEVER ...

Women did not give up their jobs easily. The number of marriages and the number of babies born both went up. But the number of married women working also went up, from 4.2 million to 6.2 million. Why was this?

Under the Nazis the German economy was booming (see page 68). By the late 1930s there was actually a shortage of workers, and women stepped into the gap. Employers liked women workers because they could pay them less. Families needed the wife's earnings as men's wages were low.

As you have already seen, the ability to use sources effectively is a crucial skill you need to practise for your GCSE History exam. Use the sample questions on this page to improve your skills. Remember to use the advice on pages 26–27 and page 57 to help you.

## Source A

An extract from a speech by Hitler at a rally in 1934:

'If one says that man's world is the State, his struggle, his readiness to devote his powers to the service of the community, one might be tempted to say that the world of woman is a smaller world. For her world is her husband, her family, her children, and her house. Only on the basis of this smaller world can the man's world be formed and built up. These two worlds are never in conflict. They are complementary to each other, they belong together as man and woman belong together.'

## Source C

The Nazi Rudolf Hess speaking in May 1936:

'We are opposed to women going into the professions which make them "mannified". What Nazis want are women who are genuine comrades and mothers. The ideal woman is one who, above all, is capable of being a mother.'

## Source B

▲ A Nazi propaganda poster from 1937

## Source D

▲ A Social Democrat Party poster produced in the elections that took place before the Nazis got into power. It says 'Women, this is what your life will be like in the Third Reich'

---

**Practice paper**

**Question 1:**

**(a)** What do Sources B and C suggest about Nazi attitudes to women? [4]

**(b)** What different view of Nazi attitudes towards women is provided in Source D? Explain your answer using Sources B, C and D. [6]

**(c)** Why do you think Sources B and C give a different view to Source D? Explain your answer using Sources B, C and D and your own knowledge. [8]

## What was the Nazi attitude towards religion?

Hitler hated Christianity. He hated its teaching of forgiveness and mercy. He hated it because it was based on the Jewish religion. Also, people who believed in God might be less likely to worship Hitler as leader of Germany. But he dared not shut the Churches down because they had such massive support among the German people. The Nazis saw the Churches as a threat. However, at first there was some co-operation between the Nazis and the Churches.

In 1933 Hitler signed a Concordat with the Catholic Church. Hitler agreed to leave the Catholic Church alone and allowed it to keep control of its schools. In return, the Catholic Church agreed to stay out of politics.

The Nazis also hoped to bring the Protestant Church under Nazi control. Hitler tried to get all the Protestant Churches to come together in one official 'Reich Church' (see page 54). The Reich Church was headed by the Protestant Bishop Ludwig Müller and had the slogan 'With the swastika on our chests and the cross in our hearts'. Reich Church pastors had to swear an oath of loyalty to Hitler. Many refused and by 1934 6000 Protestant pastors had left the Reich Church and joined a new, non-Nazi, Confessional Church.

However, Hitler was determined to control the lives and minds of young people. Therefore, in spite of his promises to leave the Churches alone, in 1936 all Church youth groups were closed down. By 1939 Church schools had also been virtually eradicated.

Hitler also encouraged an alternative religion to the Churches, the pagan German Faith Movement. This was a non-Christian movement based on worship of the sun. The movement's flag was a golden sun on a blue background, often with a Nazi swastika attached.

▲ A Nazi altar

▲ Reich Bishop Ludwig Müller making a speech in 1934

# 3.2 How successful were the Nazis in rebuilding the German economy?

**Karl**

1939

Hitler wanted to regain the land that Germany had lost in the Treaty of Versailles and to dominate Europe. To do this he needed a strong economy. The Nazis aimed to reduce unemployment and rebuild the German economy so that Germany was self-sufficient and did not rely on other countries. In this chapter you will explore how the Nazis changed the economy and the lives of German workers before reaching a judgement on how successful the Nazis' economic policies were.

> I was one of 6 million out of work in Germany in 1933. The Nazis promised to solve this problem and they did. By 1939 there was actually a shortage of workers.

## How did the Nazis change the lives of workers?

### How did the Nazis reduce unemployment?

- **By a huge building programme.** New motorways (autobahns), schools, hospitals and houses were built and paid for by the government.

- **By increasing the armed forces from 100,000 to 1,400,000.** All males aged 18–25 had to do two years' military service.

- **By re-arming Germany.** New tanks, aeroplanes, guns and battleships were ordered. Industries of all kinds, especially steel, boomed and millions of jobs were created to build these weapons.

- **By putting young men to work.** All male 18–25 year-olds did six months in the National Labour Service (RAD), doing things like planting trees or digging ditches. They were given food and lodging, but paid only pocket money.

- **By removing many women from the employment register** (see pages 62–63).

- **By removing many Jews from the employment register** (see page 75).

**Source 1**

Robert Ley, Head of the German Labour Front, speaking in May 1933:

Without the German worker there is no German nation … Workers, I swear to you that we shall not only preserve everything which exists, we shall build up even further the protection of the worker's rights, so that he can enter the new National Socialist state as a worthwhile and respected member of the nation.

**Source 2**

▲ Workers ready to start work on building the first motorway, 1933

## How were the workers treated?

Trade unions and all workers' organisations were abolished. All workers had to join the German Labour Front (DAF), run by the Nazis. The Labour Front organised some improvements to workers' lives. They negotiated better conditions at work: better lunches, new toilets, etc. Through an organisation called 'Strength Through Joy', they also arranged leisure activities for workers and their families. These included holidays (see Source 4), film-shows, concerts, hiking, keep-fit clubs and sporting fixtures. Millions of workers and their families took part.

▲ Robert Ley (see Source 1) with holidaymakers on a 'Strength Through Joy' cruiseship

▲ Young men in the National Labour Service (RAD)

## HOWEVER ...

Workers had no rights. The Labour Front did what employers asked. As a result, wages were lower and hours longer than before the Nazis came to power. Everyone had to work and skilled men could be sent to do heavy labour on schemes like autobahn building. People who refused to work under these conditions could be arrested and sent to forced labour camps. Young men in the RAD earned almost no money and were treated as if they were in the army, as you can see in Source 3.

**Activity**

1 Look back to Karl in 1933 on page 61. How do you think Nazi rule would have affected his life? In column 3 of your table list the changes that took place.
2 Mark each change out of 5 for how serious you think it is (5 = very serious, 1 = trivial).
3 Are any of the changes for the better for Karl?

# How successful were Nazi economic policies?

By 1933 the worst of the Great Depression was over. However, Germany still faced major economic problems. The huge **public buildings programme**, paid for by the government, was very successful. As you can see from Source 5, unemployment dropped dramatically. By 1939 Germany was running short of workers.

In 1936 a Four-Year Plan to get the German economy ready for war was introduced. Hermann Goering, who was also head of the German airforce, was put in charge of the plan.

As you have seen, the production of weapons, equipment and uniforms created jobs and helped to further reduce unemployment. It also boosted national pride and Hitler's popularity. The German people felt that they had finally recovered from the humiliation of the Treaty of Versailles and were now back as equals to other powerful European countries.

However, although industrial production increased, the Four-Year Plan targets were not met. Germany was not fully prepared for war by 1939. When the war started food rationing had to be introduced very quickly. Also, Germany had not become self-sufficient. It still depended on foreign imports for one-third of its raw materials.

**Source 5**

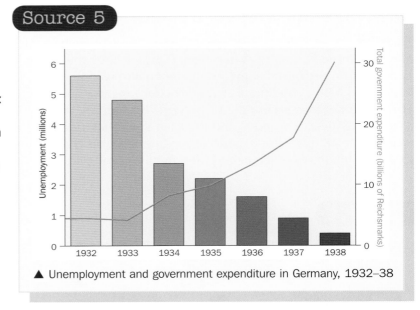

▲ Unemployment and government expenditure in Germany, 1932–38

## Activity

Did most people in Germany benefit from Nazi economic policies?
1 Where would you stand on the continuum line below? Choose three pieces of evidence to support your position.
2 Discuss your views with other students in your group. Would they stand in the same place? If not, use your key pieces of evidence to try and persuade them to move to your position.

Strongly agree                                          Strongly disagree

# What was the impact of war on the German economy and society?

The Second World War began, for Germany, in September 1939. In the early stages of the war, despite food and clothes rationing, morale amongst the German people was high as the war was going well. In 1941 German forces invaded the USSR. By the end of 1942 Hitler had achieved extraordinary military success. German forces had conquered nearly all of Europe, from the English Channel to Moscow and from northern Norway to North Africa.

However, by 1943 German forces were being driven back, in the USSR, in Africa and in southern Europe. Bad news was kept from the public by the Nazis' strict censorship, but it seeped out. Soldiers home on leave told their families and many Germans listened secretly to BBC radio broadcasts. The bombing of German cities increased. Soon they were being pounded every night by British and US bombers. There was massive destruction and homelessness to add to the other hardships. By 1944 it was clear that Germany was doomed to a terrible defeat.

By 1945 food supplies were close to running out and the German people were in a desperate state. Support for Hitler and the Nazi Party weakened. People stayed away from Nazi rallies and many refused to give the 'Heil Hitler' salute. When the war ended in May 1945 Germany was a shattered country.

## Source 6

▲ The centre of Dresden after the bombing in February 1945, which killed between 35,000 and 150,000 people in two days

## 4.1 How successful were the Nazis in influencing young people?

Hitler wanted to turn young people into loyal Nazis. In order to do so the Nazi Party set out to control all aspects of young people's lives, including their family lives, their time at school and even their leisure time. In this chapter you will explore how successful these policies were. Did the Nazis manage to influence and control all young people?

**Hans**

1939

The Nazis put a massive effort into getting us young people on their side. They knew they would never get the support of all adults, but if they could control young people they would control the future …

### Source 1

Hitler's words on youth, from *Hitler Speaks* by Herman Rauschning, 1939:

In my great educational work I am beginning with the young. My magnificent youngsters! With them I can make a new world!

My teaching is hard. Weakness has to be knocked out of them. The world will shrink in alarm from the youngsters who grow up in my schools: a violent, masterful, brave, cruel, younger generation. I will have no intellectual training. Knowledge is ruin to my young men.

## The Hitler Youth

The Hitler Youth was a successful movement even before the Nazis came to power, with 30 per cent of all young Germans already members. Once they were in power, membership became hard to avoid, with over 80 per cent of young Germans joining by 1939.

Boys joined the German Young People at the age of ten. At the age of fourteen they became members of the Hitler Youth. Here they spent their time doing physical activities such as hiking, running and jumping. They were also expected to listen to talks on Nazi political ideas and German history. To become a member of the Hitler Youth boys had to: run 60 metres in twelve seconds, jump 2.75 metres, throw a ball 25 metres, complete a one-and-a-half-day cross-country march, do close combat exercises, jump out of a first floor window wearing full army battledress and answer questions on Nazi ideas and history. One of the key aims of the Hitler Youth was to prepare boys for a life in the army by producing fit, fearless and loyal young soldiers.

## League of German Maidens

Girls joined the Young Girls at the age of ten. From the age of fourteen they were encouraged to join the League of German Maidens. For girls the emphasis was on keeping fit and home-building. To become members girls had to run 60 metres in fourteen seconds, throw a ball twelve metres, complete somersaults, a tightrope walk and a two-hour march or 100 metre swim and know how to make a bed. For girls the aim of the Hitler Youth was to prepare them for motherhood and marriage. As a result there was less emphasis on military training. However, personal fitness and loyalty were still seen as being very important.

After joining, the boy or girl swore an oath promising to love and be faithful to Hitler. Hitler Youth leaders made it clear to boys and girls that their first loyalty was to Adolf Hitler, not their family.

## Source 2

▲ Hitler Youth members jumping over fire to demonstrate their bravery

## Source 3

▲ Members of the Hitler Youth forming a swastika

# In schools

The whole curriculum was used to teach what the Nazis wanted young people to think. Teachers who refused to teach these things were sacked.

**PE:** Three double lessons a week for boys and girls. Boxing was compulsory for boys. Girls were also taught home-making and childcare.

**History:** Pupils were taught all about the unfair Treaty of Versailles, the rise of the Nazis and the wickedness of Jews and Communists. No earlier German history or history of other countries was taught.

**Biology:** Pupils were instructed on the Nazi racial ideas of the superiority of the 'Aryan race'.

**German:** Lessons focused on German war heroes and the Nazi Party.

**Geography:** Pupils were taught about the lands that had once been German and should now be re-taken.

**Maths:** Source 5 shows how Nazi ideas were put to use.

## Source 4

▲ Javelin throwers in the League of German Maidens

## Source 5

Extract from a Nazi maths textbook:

To keep a mentally ill person costs 4 marks a day. There are 300,000 mentally ill people in care.
a) How much do these people cost the state?
b) How many marriage loans [see page 62] of 1000 marks each could be made from this money?

## Activity

1   Look back to Hans in 1933 on page 61. How do you think Nazi rule would have affected his life? In column 3 of your table list the changes that took place.
2   Mark each change out of 5 for how serious you think it is (5 = very serious, 1 = trivial).
3   Are any of the changes for the better for Hans?

## Did all young people support the Nazis?

Many young people were attracted to the Hitler Youth. They enjoyed the leisure opportunities the movement offered and there was no real alternative as all other youth organisations had been made illegal.

However, others hated the Hitler Youth and one in five young Germans never joined. They found the propaganda talks boring and repetitive. They disliked being bossed about. Quite often school was cancelled to enable them to go on weekend camps (see what Hitler says about knowledge and learning in the last two sentences of Source 1, page 70) and many resented having to give up their studies. Universities complained about falling academic standards.

During the Second World War activities in the Hitler Youth became even more focused on the war effort and military training. The popularity of the Hitler Youth declined and some anti-Hitler youth movements began to appear.

## The Edelweiss Pirates

The Edelweiss Pirates were not an organised movement. It was a name used by the Nazis to classify all teenage anti-Nazi youth groups in German cities. Groups of youngsters called themselves different names in different cities: 'The Roving Dudes' in Essen; the 'Kittelbach Pirates' in Dusseldorf; the 'Navajos' in Cologne.

These rebel teenage youth groups had many similarities. They were not political opponents of the Nazis but they were determined to resist the Nazis controlling their lives. Groups tended to be made up of boys and girls aged between 14 and 17. The Pirates sang songs that made fun of Germany and they mocked and sometimes attacked Hitler Youth members.

Youth groups such as the Edelweiss Pirates angered the Nazis because they rejected the whole Nazi idea. The activities of the Edelweiss Pirates also caused problems for the Nazis in some cities. In Cologne they helped to shelter army deserters and escaped prisoners. They also stole weapons and even took part in an attack on the local Gestapo in which the chief was killed. In response the Nazis rounded up members of the Pirates and twelve were publicly hanged in November 1944 (see Source D, page 57).

Source 6

▲ An Edelweiss Pirate group who called themselves the 'Navajos'

# Meet the Examiner: Developing effective explanations – proving the importance of an event, individual or group

On page 57 we looked at the structure of Section A of the Enquiry in Depth exam.

Section B consists of three questions that are worth 24 marks in total.

- Questions (b) and (c) in this section are usually longer essay-style questions worth 8 and 12 marks (see for example pages 18–19 and page 43).

- Question (a) in Section B is different as it requires a short answer and normally carries 4 marks. It is important to make sure that your answer is short and to the point with a clear focus on the question. You do not want to be spending a long time writing a detailed explanation as you will only have 40–45 minutes to complete all three questions in Section B. You should aim to answer Question (a) in under 10 minutes.

## Sample question

> **2(a)** Why was the Hitler Youth important? [4]

## Advice: Tie what you know to the question

With only a short amount of time it is important that you make each sentence count and that you tie what you know to the question.

Avoid describing what the Hitler Youth was like.

The question is asking you to **explain why it was important**.

You need to tie specific details about what happened in the Hitler Youth to the broader context of what the Nazis wanted from young people.

## Activity

Complete the table below. Then use it to answer the sample exam question.

| Specific details: What did young people do in the Hitler Youth? |  | The Big Picture – Nazi aims |
|---|---|---|
| Boys had to jump over fire and do close combat exercises | This helped to create … | … fit and brave young soldiers who would follow orders |
| Members of the Hitler Youth learnt about German history and Nazi politics | The aim here was to ensure that members would become … | … loyal supporters of the Nazi Party |
| Girls were taught how to cook and clean | This was important because the Nazis wanted … | |
| | | |

## Further practice

You can use these questions to practise your skills at writing short, focused answers.

Remember to keep to the time limit and follow the advice above on linking what you know to the question.

- Why was hyper-inflation important? [4]
- Why was the Munich Putsch important? [4]
- Why was the SA important in Hitler's rise to power? [4]
- Why was the SS important to Hitler between 1933 and 1939? [4]

# 4.2 How important were Nazi ideas on race?

You have already seen on page 60 that Hitler and the Nazi Party had very clear ideas about the kind of Germany they wanted and the types of people they wanted living there. Only certain types of people fitted into the Nazi ideal. This chapter explores how people who did not fit into the Nazis' plans for a master race were treated and how this changed over time.

## How did the Nazis change the lives of people who did not 'fit'?

UNDESIRABLES

- *Those who **wouldn't** work.* Habitual criminals, tramps, beggars, alcoholics and others like them were regarded as socially useless. They were rounded up in 1933 and 500,000 of them were sent to concentration camps.
- *Those who **couldn't** work.* The physically disabled and mentally ill were also regarded as a burden. From 1938 onwards the Nazis began to put such people to death in gas chambers. Around 350,000 men and women who were said to produce 'inferior' offspring, or who carried inherited conditions, were compulsorily sterilised.
- *Those who did not fit into 'normal' families.* These included homosexuals, who were savagely persecuted. About 15,000 were arrested and sent to concentration camps. Many were castrated or used in medical experiments. Himmler was shocked to discover several homosexuals in the SS. He ordered them to be sent to a camp where they were 'shot while trying to escape'.
- *Those who would not make Hitler their first loyalty.* Socialists and Communists refused to do this for political reasons; Jehovah's Witnesses for religious reasons. All were put in concentration camps.
- *Those who were not 'Aryans'.* This included black people, Gypsies and Jews. Some 385 black Germans were compulsorily sterilised. Gypsies were harassed for two reasons: they were not Aryans and they did not do ordinary work. Gypsies were put in concentration camps and around 500,000 were later killed in the death camps.

Source 1

Political opponent    Habitual criminal

Jehovah's Witness    Homosexual

Gypsy    Jew

▲ These are the badges Nazis forced prisoners to wear in the concentration camps

### Activity 1

1 Look at the six groups of people listed in Source 1. Explain why each group was 'undesirable' to the Nazis.
2 Are all of these groups accepted as full members of society today? Are there any other groups who do not have full citizenship rights?

# How were Jewish people persecuted between 1933 and 1939?

Jews had suffered religious prejudice for centuries. But the Nazis took anti-Semitism to a new extreme. They used bogus research to suggest that Jews were an 'inferior' race. They blamed the Jews for the problems in Germany. They encouraged ordinary Germans to hate Jews. Gradually, they took away the civil rights of German Jews.

**Lisa**

*1939*

In 1933 there were half a million Jews in Germany. We were only about 1 per cent of the population. Not many, you might think. But Hitler was obsessed. He went after us with all the power and resources the modern German state could provide.

**Before 1933**
- Nazis encouraged boycott of Jewish-owned shops: anti-Jewish graffiti was scrawled on shop windows and members of the SA stood outside to threaten shoppers.

**1933**
- Jewish lawyers and judges dismissed.
- Jews banned from all public service jobs, such as teachers and civil servants.
- Non-Aryan children forbidden from playing with Aryan children.

**1935**
- Jewish writers not published.
- Jewish musicians barred from state orchestras.
- Jews only allowed to sit on park benches labelled 'For Jews'.
  **The Nuremberg Laws:**
  Jews could not be German citizens.
  Jews could not marry, or have sex with, non-Jews.

**1936**
- Jews not allowed to own typewriters or bicycles.
- Anti-Jewish posters temporarily removed during Berlin Olympics.

**1938**
- Jews not allowed to practise as doctors.
- Jews not allowed to run their own businesses.
- Jewish children barred from state schools.
- Jews banned from swimming pools, cinemas, theatres and concert halls.
- Male Jews had to add the name 'Israel' and females the name 'Sarah' to their own.

**1939**
- Jews not allowed to work as dentists, chemists or nurses.
- Jews' curfew: not allowed out of their homes after 8p.m. in winter, 9p.m. in summer.
- Jews to hand over any jewellery, gold or silver to the police.

## Discuss

Look at the restrictions listed in the timeline above. Which ones:
- were minor nuisances
- prevented Jewish children from having a normal childhood
- prevented Jews from earning a living
- were serious restrictions on Jews' rights as citizens of Germany?

## Activity 2

Complete the table for Lisa that you began for the activity on page 60.

# 4.3 From persecution to genocide: how did the Nazi treatment of Jews change during the Second World War?

Hitler's own anti-Semitism was deep-rooted. You have already seen how the Nazis made life increasingly difficult for the Jews of Germany from the moment they took power in 1933. But the Second World War allowed the Nazis to push their anti-Jewish policy to new extremes.

## The ghettos

After Germany invaded Poland on 1 September 1939, another 3.5 million Jews were trapped under Nazi rule. In Poland, Jews were forced into special sections of cities, called ghettos. The largest ghetto in Poland was the Warsaw ghetto. The ghetto was shut off from the rest of the city – if Jews tried to escape they were executed. It was also impossibly over-crowded. Water and power were cut off and food was very limited. People had to survive on just 300 calories a day (the equivalent of two and a half slices of bread). Jews who could work were used for slave labour. Those who could not were left to die from hunger and disease. Over half a million Jews died in the Warsaw ghetto.

### Source 1

▲ Young children in the Warsaw ghetto, 1941

### Source 2

▲ An Einsatzgrüppe soldier about to shoot a Jew at a mass grave in Vinnitsa, in what is now Ukraine

## The Einsatzgrüppen

By the end of 1941 the German army had invaded a large part of the Soviet Union as well as Poland. Six million Jews were now living in territory controlled by the Germans. As the German army advanced through Eastern Europe it was followed by special SS units called Einsatzgrüppen. The job of these units was to murder Communists, Jews and other people classed as 'undesirables'. They rounded up Jews in each town, took them out into the country nearby and ordered them to dig a trench. The Jews were then shot and fell into the trench which became a mass grave.

# The 'Final Solution'

On 31 July 1941, Goering (the Economics Minister) ordered Himmler (the Head of the SS) and Heydrich (an SS general) to carry out the 'final solution' to the 'Jewish question' in Europe. Shooting (carried out by the Einsatzgrüppen) and the ghettos were seen as 'inefficient' ways of killing millions of people.

In January 1942 Nazi leaders held a conference at Wannsee, near Berlin, to work out a more 'efficient' way of killing Jews. It was decided to bring in industrial methods. Six special death camps were built. All had good railway links, so Jews could be brought by train from all over Europe – a terrible journey of several days. Many died on the way.

Auschwitz was one of these camps, and began killing people by the end of 1941. By the end of the war, 1,100,000 people had been killed in the Auschwitz gas chambers. The other camps were:

- **Treblinka:** at this tiny camp, only 600 metres by 400 metres, at least 850,000 Jews, mainly from Warsaw but also from elsewhere in Europe, including Hungary and Greece, were killed, as well as over 2000 Gypsies and Roma.

- **Sobibor:** at least 300,000 Jews as well as thousands of Soviet prisoners of war were killed.

- **Belzec:** at least 600,000 Jews, mainly from Poland, and several thousand Gypsies were killed here.

- **Majdenek:** 60,000 Jews from all over Europe, as well as non-Jewish Poles and Russians, were killed here.

- **Chelmno:** over 150,000 Jews were killed here.

These death camps were different from the 15 concentration camps (see Source 3), that the Nazis had used right from 1933 to imprison their enemies. Concentration camps were not built to kill people, although many thousands died in them, of brutality, disease and starvation.

Source 3

▲ Map showing concentration and death camps and major 'euthanasia centres'

77

# Case Study: Auschwitz death camp

The Nazis were proud of their efficient death machine. In every country that the Nazis ruled, lists of Jews were drawn up. They were taken from their homes and put on trains. On arrival at the camp inmates walked past a Nazi doctor who indicated whether they should go left or right: left to work; right to the gas chambers. About 80 per cent of arrivals were killed at once; those put to work normally lasted just a few months before dying of malnutrition and overwork. Source 4 describes how the killings were carried out.

By the end of the war some six million Jews had been murdered, as well as Gypsies, homosexuals and around 4 million Russian prisoners of war.

## Source 4

An extract from the memoirs of Rudolph Höss, commandant of Auschwitz, written after his arrest. He was tried for war crimes and executed in 1947:

Before entering the gas chamber, Jewish prisoners would tell them in their own language to leave their clothes neatly together and remember where they had put them.

The women went in first with the children, followed by the men … The door would be quickly screwed up and the gas released through vents in the ceiling. About one-third died straightaway. The remainder began to scream and struggle for air. The screaming, however, soon changed to the death rattle and in a few minutes all lay still. It took from three to fifteen minutes to kill everybody.

We usually waited about half-an-hour before we opened the doors. The bodies were then taken up by lift and laid in front of the ovens which had been stoked up. Up to three corpses could be put in each oven at the same time.

## Source 5

▲ A gas chamber in Auschwitz death camp. The gas used was Zyklon B, a cyanide poison gas. It took up to 15 minutes to kill everybody

## Source 6

▲ The entrance to the Auschwitz death camp, where more than one million people were killed during the Second World War. Note the train tracks leading right into the camp. Trains brought Jews to Auschwitz from all over Nazi-occupied Europe

# How did the Jews resist?

## Jewish partisan groups

Jews did fight against what was happening to them. Jewish resistance groups took to the countryside. In Poland there were at least 28 groups of Jewish fighters. These resistance groups blew up railway lines and attacked German soldiers. During 1942 as many as 40,000 Jews escaped from the ghettos of Poland into the forests. They had hardly any weapons and their main source of food was what the forests could provide. The German army was forced to use large numbers of men and even aircraft against them.

## Uprisings in the ghettos

Armed uprisings took place in many ghettos. In 1943, in the Warsaw ghetto, 15,000 Jews armed with makeshift weapons held out for four weeks against fully equipped German forces. Street by street the Germans set fire to dynamited buildings until the ghetto was reduced to rubble. Seven thousand Jews were killed in the fighting.

## Uprisings in the camps

There were also uprisings in the camps. In Treblinka, in 1943, one of the prisoners managed to get into the weapons store. He handed out grenades and guns to other prisoners. The camp was set on fire: 15 guards were killed and 150 prisoners managed to escape. In October 1943, 600 Jews escaped from Sobibor camp in Poland. In Auschwitz Jews managed to blow up two of the gas chambers.

**Source 7**

▲ Members of a Jewish partisan unit in the Parczew Forest

## Activity

Look at this list of people who helped to make the Holocaust happen:
- Hitler
- Hitler's henchmen, such as Himmler and Goebbels
- camp commandants, such as Rudolph Höss (see Source 4)
- the SS camp doctors who made the selection
- the clerks who wrote the lists of Jews' names
- the police who rounded up the Jews
- the engine drivers who drove the trains to the camps
- the engineers who designed the gas chambers
- the builders who built the gas chambers
- the German people who did nothing to stop the killings
- governments of other countries who didn't bomb the railway lines and camps.

1 Are all these people to blame?
2 Who is most to blame?
3 Who could have stopped the Holocaust?

# Meet the Examiner: Planning your approach to essay-style questions

On page 43 we looked at the final question that you will have to answer on your exam paper. This question carries the most marks and needs to be planned very carefully. In the case of the sample exam question below you need to weigh the importance of the Second World War as a factor in changing Nazi policies towards the Jews against other factors.

Some events are so important that they can be called '**turning points**' in history. A turning point is different from a **catalyst** (which speeds up changes that are already taking place). A turning point is more important because it changes the direction of the way things are going.

For many people the start of the Second World War marks the key turning point in the way that the Nazis treated the Jews. It changed the direction of Nazi policy from persecution to genocide. Do you agree? Was the Second World War a turning point or were other factors more important?

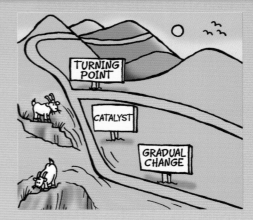

> How important was the Second World War, amongst other factors, in changing Nazi policies towards the Jews? [12]

## Planning your answer

There are 12 marks available for this question. You will not gain a high level mark if your answer only explains how the Second World War changed Nazi policies. Remember to avoid hitting the iceberg by making sure you explore both sides of the argument. You should aim for three paragraphs.

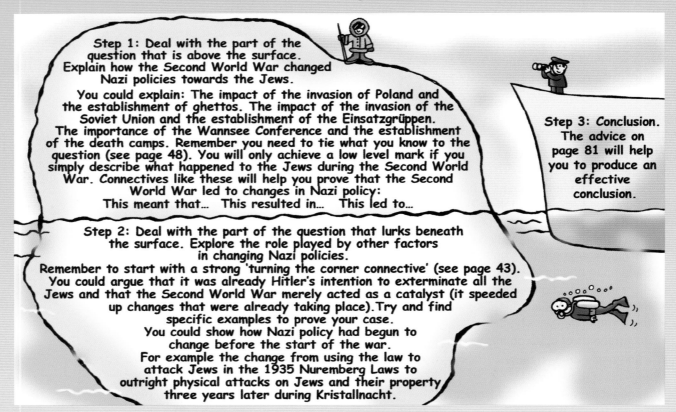

**Step 1:** Deal with the part of the question that is above the surface. Explain how the Second World War changed Nazi policies towards the Jews.

You could explain: The impact of the invasion of Poland and the establishment of ghettos. The impact of the invasion of the Soviet Union and the establishment of the Einsatzgrüppen. The importance of the Wannsee Conference and the establishment of the death camps. Remember you need to tie what you know to the question (see page 48). You will only achieve a low level mark if you simply describe what happened to the Jews during the Second World War. Connectives like these will help you prove that the Second World War led to changes in Nazi policy:
This meant that... This resulted in... This led to...

**Step 2:** Deal with the part of the question that lurks beneath the surface. Explore the role played by other factors in changing Nazi policies.
Remember to start with a strong 'turning the corner connective' (see page 43). You could argue that it was already Hitler's intention to exterminate all the Jews and that the Second World War merely acted as a catalyst (it speeded up changes that were already taking place). Try and find specific examples to prove your case.
You could show how Nazi policy had begun to change before the start of the war.
For example the change from using the law to attack Jews in the 1935 Nuremberg Laws to outright physical attacks on Jews and their property three years later during Kristallnacht.

**Step 3:** Conclusion. The advice on page 81 will help you to produce an effective conclusion.

# Meet the Examiner: Writing effective conclusions

The conclusion is a crucial part of your answer. Some students forget to add a conclusion or produce a weak ending to their answer. You have been asked to **evaluate** how important the Second World War was as a factor in changing Nazi policies towards the Jews. You need to be confident and **reach an overall judgement**.

Imagine that you could put the evidence on scales. On one side is evidence to support the view that the Second World War was the most important factor that changed the way that Jews were treated. On the other side is evidence of other factors playing a role in changing Nazi policies. Which way would the scales tip? Which side has the strongest evidence to support it? Was the Second World War a turning point?

## What makes an effective conclusion?

### Things to avoid

- A detailed summary of everything that has already been said.
- A one-sentence conclusion which reaches an overall judgement but does not explain it or show that there are two sides to the argument.
- A weak conclusion, that sits on the fence and does not reach an overall judgement.

### Things to do

- Show that you recognise that there is evidence that agrees and disagrees with the statement.
- Come to a strong overall judgement.
- Explain your main reason for reaching this judgement.

## How to structure a conclusion

Start by conceding that the weaker argument has some strengths.

↓

Give an example.

↓

Then make it clear that the other argument is stronger.

↓

Provide your main piece(s) of evidence that supports this.

↓

Try to end with a memorable final sentence.

### Example 1

The Second World War did play a role in changing Nazi policies towards the Jews.

↓

For example ...

↓

However, other factors played a more important role.

↓

This is because ...

↓

The Second World War was a catalyst that speeded up changes that were already taking place.

### Example 2

The Second World War was not the only factor that changed Nazi policies towards the Jews. Other events were also important.

↓

For example ...

↓

However, overall the Second World War was the most important factor.

↓

This is because ...

↓

The Second World War was the crucial turning point, changing the direction of Nazi policy from persecution to genocide.

## 5.1 How did the Nazis change the cultural climate of Weimar Germany?

In the 1920s a lively, modern culture developed under the Weimar Republic. In this section you will explore the art and entertainment that existed in the 1920s. You will need to work out why the Nazis disapproved of Weimar culture and were so keen to change the cultural climate of Germany when they took control.

### Art and entertainment during the 1920s

With peace at home and abroad, and a new prosperity – for some at least, Germany under the Weimar Republic experienced a cultural revival during the 1920s. Writers, poets, artists and film-makers flourished. Artists such as Grosz, Klee and Kandinsky had international reputations, while Berlin became famous for its jazz bands and daring cabaret acts. Going to clubs was a major pastime. By 1927 there were over 700 jazz bands in Berlin.

Before the First World War there had been strict censorship in Germany. However, during the time of the Weimar Republic restrictions were removed. Cabaret artists performed songs criticising the government, sex was discussed openly and Berlin became famous for its transvestite balls, naked dancing and nightclubs.

The 1920s were a golden age for the German film industry. Films made by German directors such as Fritz Lang were technically advanced and attracted large audiences. Actresses like Marlene Dietrich became very popular, playing strong and glamorous female characters.

In modern architecture the Bauhaus school led the world. Bauhaus architects made use of modern materials like steel and plate glass to design new and exciting houses, apartments, factories, galleries and shops.

However, not everyone approved of the cultural revival that took place during the 1920s. Some thought that Weimar culture represented a moral decline and that things had gone too far. They were shocked by the club scene in Berlin and argued for a return to simple, traditional values. The Nazis felt the same.

Source 1

▲ A poster for the film *The Blue Angel*, starring Marlene Dietrich. The story focuses on a university professor who becomes obsessed with a cabaret singer called Lola

82

# How did the Nazis change Weimar culture?

The Nazis ended the free expression that had existed during the time of the Weimar government. They introduced strict controls. No books could be produced without permission and only Nazi-approved artists could show their work.

## Music and theatre

Jazz music was banned because it was seen as 'black' music which was racially inferior. The Nazis preferred German folk music, marching songs and classical music by German composers such as Bach, Beethoven and Mozart. Theatre productions that focused on German history and politics were encouraged.

## Art

Hitler took a particular interest in art and architecture. In his early years he had tried to earn a living as an artist. He had very firm views of what kind of art should be produced. He disliked the kind of 'modern' art produced during the 1920s. He thought that much of it was perverted and unpatriotic. Hitler wanted art to glorify the 'Master Race' and celebrate healthy, strong Aryans. He preferred paintings or sculptures showing heroic-looking Aryans, military figures or images of the ideal Aryan family. In 1937 the Nazis opened the House of German Art to show officially approved art.

## Architecture

Hitler believed that architecture could influence people's lives. He favoured two styles of building:

- the 'monumental style' for public buildings. These were large and built of stone. The design was similar to Greek and Roman public buildings with lots of columns and steps
- the 'country style' for family homes. These were traditional-style German buildings using wood and stone, and with shutters and pitched roofs.

### Activity

1 Why would Hitler and other leading Nazis have disapproved of the arts and entertainment produced during the 1920s?
2 Look at Sources 2 and 3. Why would Hitler have approved of these examples of art and architecture?

▲ *Kahlenberg farmer and his family*, a painting from 1939

▲ Architect's model of the Konigsplatz in Munich

# 5.2 How did the Nazis use propaganda to control the German people?

As we have already seen in Section 2.2, Heinrich Himmler used his terror network to keep the German people in line. However, the Nazis did not just use fear to control the German people. Josef Goebbels, another important henchman, ran the Nazis' propaganda network. This chapter explores the methods that Goebbels used to control the German people through propaganda. Was he more important than any other henchman?

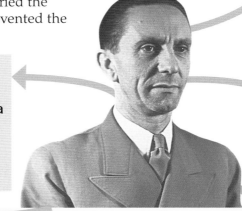

> ### Source 1
>
> From *Mein Kampf*, by Adolf Hitler:
>
> The powers of understanding of the masses are feeble. And they quickly forget. So effective propaganda has to be limited to a few bare essentials and these must be as simple as possible. These slogans should be repeated until the very last person has come to grasp the idea.

## Control by propaganda?

In 1924 Hitler laid out his beliefs and his plans for successful propaganda in his book, *Mein Kampf* (see Source 1). In 1928 he chose Josef Goebbels to run the Nazi Ministry of Propaganda.

Goebbels put Hitler's approach to propaganda into practice brilliantly. He took control of all the mass media. He made sure newspapers and posters carried the strong, simple, repeated slogans of the Nazis. Through censorship he prevented the German people from hearing any conflicting messages.

### Newspapers

Anti-Nazi newspapers were shut down. Jews were banned from owning or working for newspapers. Goebbels' Ministry of Propaganda sent out daily instructions to all remaining newspapers telling them what to print, what kind of pictures should be published and what angle they should take on the news. Display boards were set up in public places so that everyone could read these newspapers.

### Rallies

### Source 2

The Nazis always presented an image of order and control to the German people, with their uniforms, meetings, torchlight processions and rallies. Once they were in power, they made their rallies even more impressive. A huge stadium at Nuremberg was specially built for them (see Source 2). Goebbels stage-managed these rallies to give a dramatic impression of overwhelming power and unity.

◄ Nuremberg rally, 1937. There are 100,000 Nazis here, with 32,000 flags

## Books

As soon as they came to power, the Nazis organised official book-burnings – books were burned in public on massive bonfires. The Nazis burned:

- books by Communists and Socialists
- books by Jews
- books by anyone they disapproved of
- books containing ideas they disapproved of.

By burning books the Nazis were preventing German people from reading and thinking beyond the Nazi message. All new books published had to be censored by Goebbels' Ministry.

▲ Book-burning, 1933

## Radio

Goebbels took over control of all radio broadcasting. Regular programmes included Hitler's speeches, German music and German history – foreign programmes could not be picked up. Cheap radios were made so that as many Germans as possible could listen to Nazi propaganda. By 1939 70 per cent of Germans owned a radio. Loudspeakers were set up in public squares all over Germany and people were encouraged to listen to important radio programmes and announcements.

Newspaper advertisement, 1934:

Attention! The Führer is speaking on the radio! On Wednesday 21 March, the Führer is speaking on all German stations from 11.00a.m. to 11.50a.m. Nazi Party headquarters have ordered that all factory-owners, department stores, offices, shops, pubs and blocks of flats put up loudspeakers an hour before the broadcast so that the whole workforce can participate fully in the broadcast.

▲ A Dutch poster for *The Eternal Jew* (in German, *Der ewige Jude*), 1940

## Films

The cinema was very popular in most countries in the 1930s. Goebbels controlled all of the films made in Germany. Most were adventure stories, comedies or love stories, but there was always a newsreel film, *News of the Week*. The newsreels were made by Goebbels' film-makers and shown before the main film.

Some openly pro-Nazi films were made on Goebbels' orders and with strict control of the scripts. Source 5 is a poster for *The Eternal Jew*, an anti-Semitic film made by the Nazis.

**Activity**

Which propaganda method do you think was the **most** important? Use the Meet the Examiner advice on page 73 to help you prove your case.

# Sport as propaganda: the 1936 Berlin Olympics

One of Goebbels' greatest propaganda challenges came when Berlin was selected as the venue for the 1936 Olympic Games. Some leading Nazis did not want Germany to host the Olympics but Goebbels argued that it would be a great propaganda opportunity.

Goebbels aimed to use the Olympics to:

- improve the reputation of Germany abroad – by presenting it as a modern, well-organised and civilised society
- show that the Aryan race was superior to all other races
- increase German national pride, thereby making Hitler and the Nazi Party more popular.

Goebbels built a brand new stadium (see Source 6) and made full use of the latest technology available. He brought in television cameras for the first time and the most sophisticated electronic timing device was installed. The stadium had the largest stop clock ever built. Many visitors were impressed with how well organised the Games were and with the modern facilities for athletes and spectators. However, the heavy presence of army and SS soldiers who patrolled the stadium or stood on guard did not make a favourable impression on some visitors.

> **Activity**
>
> To what extent were the Berlin Olympics a propaganda success for Goebbels? Use the information and sources on pages 86–87 to evaluate the extent to which Goebbels achieved all of his aims.

## Source 6

▲ The Olympic Stadium in Berlin. This could hold 100,000 people and was lit by the most modern electric lighting

## Source 7

R. Hart-Davis, *Hitler's Games*, 1986:

Everyone who saw the opening ceremony agreed that it had been magnificently planned and executed. Foreign visitors were astonished and not a little unnerved by the colossal scale of the stadium and all the arrangements – by the huge number of soldiers lining the route to the stadium, by the continuous saluting. Another feature that shook visitors was the hysterical adulation accorded to the Führer [Hitler] wherever he went; men who saw him yelled themselves hoarse, women gave piercing screams, wept with excitement, fainted.

Television was in its infancy; and this was the first occasion on which it was used to cover a sporting function. The pictures were scarcely recognisable, many people turned away in disappointment. Television apart, the technical facilities were faultless. The photo-electric timing mechanism worked perfectly and a constant source of fascination for the crowd was the immense stopwatch mounted on the Marathon Gate, the largest stopwatch ever built.

## Source 8

William E. Dodd, U.S. Ambassador to Germany, describing the closing ceremony. Dodd was opposed to Nazism:

I have never seen such an elaborate show. How much the Olympics cost one can hardly imagine, though I would guess 75 million marks. The propaganda of it may have pleased the Germans. It had a bad influence on foreigners, as reported to me, in spite of the fine entertainment of all concerned.

## Source 9

Godfrey Brown, a 400-metre runner in the British team, 1936:

The fact is that some of us went to Berlin with a mistaken idea – that we were going to take place in a sports meeting. Instead we were treated to a piece of political propaganda. On the last day we were inflicted with the sight of thousands of gross, flabby Germans, so-called Hitler Youth, clad in nothing but shorts and performing ridiculous evolutions on the grass. We cried, 'Sweep on, you fat and greasy citizens' and made a dash for the first train home.

Hitler's persecution of the Jews was well known by this time. Some countries threatened to boycott the Games. In response the Nazis included one token Jewish athlete in their team. Other countries sent amateur athletes who had to take time off work and lose pay to attend the Games. In contrast, German competitors were full-time athletes and had trained carefully for the Games. Germany topped the medals table, winning 33 gold medals (nine more than the United States who came second). However, the star of the Games was Jesse Owens, a black American athlete, who won four gold medals and broke eleven world records in doing so. The ten black members of the American team won 13 medals between them.

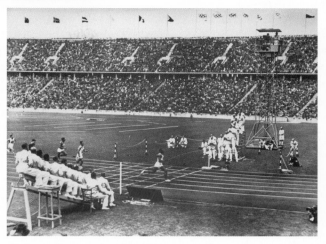

**Source 10**

▲ Jesse Owens wins the 100 metres. Owens was popular with the German crowd. He won gold medals in the 100 metres, 200 metres, long jump and 4x100 metres relay

## smarter revision

### Using flash cards to summarise key topics

**Activity**

Who was the most important of Hitler's henchmen: Heinrich Himmler (see pages 50–51), Hermann Goering (see page 68) or Josef Goebbels (see pages 84–85)?

Name: Josef Goebbels
Position: In charge of the Nazi Ministry of Propaganda
Methods:
* Newspapers
* Rallies
Why important?

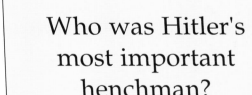

Who was Hitler's most important henchman?

1 Prepare a **flash card** on each henchman. Flash cards are a very useful way to revise a topic. They should contain the key information about an individual or event. You should use sub-headings or key questions to structure the information on the card.

2 Prepare a speech for a class debate in which you **prove** that the individual you have chosen was the most important. Simply describing what the individual did will not win you the argument.

# Meet the Examiner: Producing a time plan

On page 57 you saw how Section A on your Enquiry in Depth exam paper will be structured. It is important to note that the last two questions carry as many marks as the first three. You need to time yourself very carefully during the exam. It is worth producing a time plan like the one below.

> *TIME PLAN*
> *Section A (1 hour)*
> *Questions 1–3: 30 minutes*
> *Questions 4–5: 30 minutes*
> *Section B (40 minutes)*
> *Questions 1–2: 20 minutes*
> *Question 3: 20 minutes*
> *Check answers for spelling, punctuation and grammar (5 minutes)*
> *\* If time is short, check the last questions in Sections A (1e) and B (2c or 3c) first as these carry the most marks.*

## Activity

Allow yourself 30 minutes to answer the two sample exam questions below. Use the advice on page 89 to help you answer question 1(d). For question 1(e) refer back to pages 48–49 which provide advice on how to approach this type of question.

**1(d)** How useful is Source A for understanding how foreign visitors reacted to the Berlin Olympics in 1936? Explain your answer using Source A and your own knowledge. [8]

**1(e)** How did the Nazis use propaganda to control the lives of the German people? [10]

## Source A

William E. Dodd, U.S. Ambassador to Germany, describing the closing ceremony. Dodd was opposed to Nazism:

I have never seen such an elaborate show. How much the Olympics cost one can hardly imagine, though I would guess 75 million marks. The propaganda of it may have pleased the Germans. It had a bad influence on foreigners, as reported to me, in spite of the fine entertainment of all concerned.

# Meet the Examiner: Evaluating the usefulness of sources

In your exam paper, questions will often be set that ask you to evaluate the value of a source for a specific enquiry. This question requires you to evaluate the extent to which the information in a source would help the historian in a specific enquiry and how reliable that information is. You need to think carefully about how you approach this type of question.

Often students answer utility questions by either commenting on:
- the relevance of the information contained in the source

*or*
- the reliability of the source.

You must aim to do both!

Consider the content **and** the reliability of the source.

You also need to consider the strengths **and** weaknesses of the source.

REMEMBER … the question is asking you how useful the sources are, not how useless they are. There will not be any sources that are completely useless. Do not get bogged down telling the examiner what is wrong with the source. Try to begin and end your answer positively.

Use the planning grid below to help you develop an effective answer.

- Do not worry if you cannot fill in all sections of the table. It is a planning tool to help you get started and to get you thinking.
- Remember to support your comments with evidence from the source.

| | Strengths | Weaknesses |
|---|---|---|
| **STEP 1: CONSIDER CONTENT**<br>(a) **What do we learn?** (Use your inference skills)<br>Consider the source's CONTENT but do not fall into the trap of repeating what the source says in your own words.<br>Explain how the source can be used.<br>Explain why it contains useful information.<br><br>(b) **What do we not learn?**<br>What is missed out?<br>What else would you want to know? | **Source A is useful because** it helps us understand …<br><br>We also learn that … | **However, Source A has some limitations.** It does not provide us with information on … |
| **STEP 2: CONSIDER THE PROVENANCE OF THE SOURCE**<br>What is the **nature** of the source? What type of source is it?<br>What are the **origins** of the source? Who wrote or produced it? When was it produced?<br>What was the **purpose** of the source? Why was it produced? | Source A is a …<br>The advantage of this is … | However, we need to be careful about totally trusting the impression given in Source A. This is because … |
| **STEP 3: COMPARE TO OTHER SOURCES AND YOUR OWN KNOWLEDGE**<br>**How typical** is the source?<br>Did others react in the same way? | Source A is typical of the reaction of many visitors. For example … | However, not all visitors reacted in this way. Some … |
| **STEP 4: REACH AN OVERALL JUDGEMENT**<br>Students often fail to reach an overall evaluation. Make sure you do not forget a conclusion that really addresses the question.<br><br>**Always** end with a CONCLUSION in which you reach a judgement.<br>• **How useful** is the source (very/quite)?<br>• What is your key reason for reaching this judgement? | | |

# Smarter Revision: Putting it all together

This book has suggested some strategies you could use to help you revise. Here is a reminder of them. When you come to revise, remember that each one can be used for any topic.

## Memory maps

Memory maps are an excellent way to summarise your notes and boost your memory. At the end of Section 1.1 you produced a memory map to summarise the problems faced by the Weimar Republic. You can use memory maps to summarise other key topics.

### Activity 1

Use the advice on pages 20–21 to produce a memory map that summarises how Hitler used terror and propaganda to control Germany (see Sections 2.2 and 5.2). You could start like this:

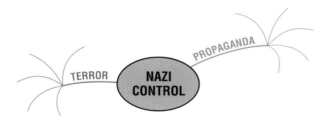

## Acronyms

We used a LAMB on page 20 to help you remember the terms of the Treaty of Versailles. You also made your own acronym to remember the problems faced by the Weimar Republic. Here is another one to sum up Hitler's BIG ideas for how Germany should be ruled.

**B**lood – Hitler believed that only those of 'pure German **blood**' should be part of the Master Race. This idea led to the persecution of the Jews and, eventually, the Holocaust.

**I**nvasion – Hitler thought that Germany should **invade** other countries in order to provide 'living space' for the growing German population. This idea led to the Second World War.

**G**overnment – Hitler believed in strong **government**. This led to the destruction of democracy and the establishment of a dictatorship.

### Activity 2

The best acronyms are the ones you make up yourself. If you create it yourself it is easier to remember. Work in pairs. Invent an acronym to help you remember another topic, for example the reasons why opposition to the Nazis was weak (see pages 58–59). Vote in class on the best acronym.

# Living graphs

Living graphs can help summarise topics in a way that actively engages your brain. Look at the living graph you produced in Section 2.1 (see page 45) to explore how Hitler became a dictator. Most students would find it easier to remember the graph in an exam than a list of bullet points. You could use a similar method to sort out the key points in Sections 1.3 and 1.4.

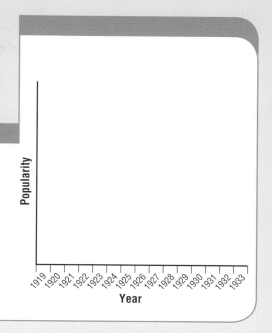

## Activity 3

1 Produce a living graph like this which plots the popularity of the Nazi Party from 1919 to 1933.
2 Produce a living graph which plots the popularity of the Weimar Republic from 1919 to 1933.
3 Compare the two graphs. What pattern can you see?

You could also convert this into a 'walking graph'. Mark out the graph on the floor and you and your class become the graph. Your teacher can tell you how to do this. It is often easier to remember something active that you have done.

# Flash cards

Key events or topics can be summarised on small cards like this:

## Activity 4

1 Work in groups. Produce flash cards on the key events and key individuals you need to revise for the exam.
2 Work in groups. Each person in the group writes 26 questions – two quiz questions on each of the thirteen key sections in this book. Use your quiz to test other people in your group.
3 Design a revision game for Germany 1919–1945. You could produce it in the style of *Who Wants To Be A Millionaire?*, where the questions gradually get harder, or in the style of the *Weakest Link*.

# Quizzes

You need to test yourself regularly during the run-up to the exam. If you do not trust yourself, get someone else to test you! Revision doesn't have to be boring. Try to make it as much fun as possible by designing quizzes and games.

## Using tables to organise your revision

Making tables helps you to remember the key points.

Use the information from pages 70–71 to copy and complete this table about how young people's lives changed under the Nazis. Some boxes have already been filled in for you. Use the Results column to consider whether people's lives changed as much as the Nazis would have liked. The paragraph that starts 'However …' on page 72 will help you.

> **Activity 1**
>
> Make your own versions of the table below that summarise how life changed for workers, women and Jewish people.

| Young people | Situation in 1933 | Changes the Nazis made up to 1939 | Results |
|---|---|---|---|
| **School** | | Nazi control of the curriculum. Teachers had to obey. Many subjects were changed to include putting across Nazi ideas; for example … | |
| **Leisure** | Could choose how they spent their leisure time. | | |

## Using pictures to trigger your memory

Another way of organising, learning and remembering the changes in people's lives under the Nazis is to look at Hans, Gudrun, Karl and Lisa (see page 61).

Here is Gudrun in 1933 and 1939. Fill in the boxes with notes about each aspect of Gudrun's life in 1933 and 1939.

> **Activity 2**
>
> Make and label your own sketches for Hans, Karl and Lisa in the same way.

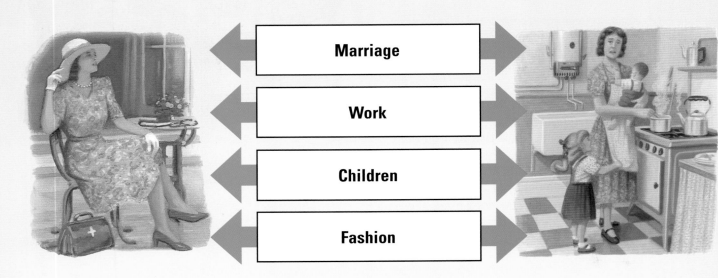

- Marriage
- Work
- Children
- Fashion

# Glossary

**ALLIES** countries that have signed an agreement to support each other

**ANTI-SEMITISM** hatred of Jews

**ARMISTICE** cease-fire agreement

**ARYAN** Nazi word for the German 'race'

**ATTRIBUTION** information given with a historical source describing who produced it, when, why, etc.

**CONSTITUTION** the rules that decide how a country is governed

**DAWES PLAN** an agreement between the USA and European countries in 1924, drawn up for the USA by Charles Dawes. The plan organised US loans to revive European economies, especially that of Germany

**DEMOCRACY** a system of government in which all adults have the right to vote for the government they want

**EMERGENCY POWERS** the right of the German President to act outside the normal rules of the constitution in a crisis

**ENABLING ACT** the Enabling Act was passed in 1933, giving Hitler power to act without consulting the Reichstag or the President

**EXTREMIST PARTIES** groups holding extreme political views. In Germany at this time the Nazis and the Communists were extremist parties seeking to overthrow democracy

**FREIKORPS** organisation of armed ex-soldier volunteers

**FÜHRER** the German word for leader. Hitler's title after the death of President Hindenburg in 1934

**GERMAN LABOUR FRONT (DAF)** an organisation set up by the Nazis to improve the lives of workers

**HYPER-INFLATION** inflation is when money decreases in value, so more is needed to pay for the same things. Hyper-inflation is where this gets completely out of control and prices rise by enormous amounts

**KAISER** German Emperor (the last Kaiser's rule ended in 1918)

**LEAGUE OF NATIONS** set up in 1919 for the promotion of international peace and security. Germany was a member from 1926 to 1933

**PASSIVE RESISTANCE** opposing government action in non-violent ways, refusing to co-operate, staging strikes, etc.

**PROPORTIONAL REPRESENTATION (PR)** a system of elections in which the number of people elected for a party is in proportion to the number of votes for that party. It gives representation to minorities, who do not do well in the 'first past the post' system, which is used in Britain today. PR can lead to lots of small parties and unstable governments

**PUTSCH** an armed uprising aimed at taking over the government

**REICHSTAG** German parliament

**REPARATIONS** compensation for the damage caused by the First World War demanded by the victorious Allies from Germany on the grounds that Germany was to blame for the war (by Article 231 of the Treaty of Versailles). The amount was fixed at £6.6 million in 1921 but nothing like this amount was ever paid

**REPUBLIC** a state that has an elected head of state rather than a hereditary ruler

**SA** abbreviation for Stürm-Abteilung (Stormtroopers). The brown-shirted gangs set up by Hitler to protect his meetings and break up the meetings of opponents in the early days of the Nazi Party

**SS** abbreviation for Schutz Staffel (protection squad). Originally Hitler's private bodyguard, they wore black uniforms and swore a personal oath of loyalty to him

**WALL STREET CRASH** sudden fall in stock prices in June 1929 on the US stock exchange, in Wall Street, New York

**YOUNG PLAN** an agreement made between Germany and the Allies, named after US representative Young, to lower reparations and allow Germany to pay them back over a longer period

# Index